Politics and Privilege
in a Mexican City

Stanford Studies in Comparative Politics, 5

Politics and Privilege
in a Mexican City

Richard R. Fagen and
William S. Tuohy

Stanford University Press
Stanford, California

Stanford University Press
Stanford, California
© 1972 by the Board of Trustees of the
Leland Stanford Junior University
Printed in the United States of America
Cloth ISBN 0-8047-0809-6
Paper ISBN 0-8047-0879-7
Original edition 1972
Last figure below indicates year of this printing:
84 83 82 81 80 79 78 77 76 75

Preface

From one developmental perspective, the achievements of modern Mexico are impressive indeed. With its aggregate economic growth, its well institutionalized practices of rule and succession, and its effective management of conflict, Mexico has often been held up as a model for other developing nations, its achievements collectively celebrated as *el milagro mexicano*.

Mexican political elites have made civic peace and stability their primary goal, creating and maintaining a complex and finely tuned government/Party apparatus for this purpose. Second only to political stability has been the goal of maximum economic growth, to be achieved by encouraging private capital to invest in industrial development. State intervention in the economy has been selective, not pervasive. The economy continues to expand, and the political regime remains strong and stable despite intermittent challenges in state and local elections, sporadic acts of resistance by small leftist groups, and frequent but isolated *campesino* protests over land ownership, commodity prices, and agricultural credit.

Furthermore, the outcomes and consequences of these political and economic arrangements have been embraced not only by those who have most obviously profited from them, but also by substantial numbers of people who obviously have not profited from them at all. Elites have been relatively successful in generating acceptance, if not always enthusiastic support, of the national regime. Their refusal to permit increased political participation and competition is recognized as necessary by many Mexicans and openly welcomed by some. Even disappointments and hardships stemming from acute economic deprivation are frequently explained away or simply overlooked in a diffuse mood of optimism.

It is with this general map of Mexican society and politics that we have approached Jalapa, capital city of the coastal state of Veracruz. Thus our concern in writing about Jalapan politics is not only with Harold Lasswell's "who gets what, when, and how," but also with who doesn't get what and why. In particular, we have emphasized the cumulative nature of political, economic, and social privilege in Jalapa, the patterns of citizen belief and behavior that sustain existing institutions, and the political quiescence and stability that result from this perpetuation of the status quo. Additionally, we have considered the normative implications of the Jalapeño political system: the question who *ought* to get what, when, and how—or at least where one might begin in trying to design more nearly equitable alternatives to existing arrangements.

We aspire to a relevance and a readership wider than our focus on a medium-sized Mexican city might suggest, for we see in Jalapa not only a microcosm of the Mexican political system, but also a reflection of bureaucratic and authoritarian politics in general. If at times we seem harsh in our descriptions and evaluations of the governance of Jalapa, it is not our intent to mock or expose either its leaders or its citizens, but merely to report things as we see them. Precisely because the regime under which Jalapeños live is the common lot of millions of people in poor and not-so-poor countries alike, it deserves to be more widely known. We seek a more profound understanding of the workings of such systems in the hope that some day not only Jalapeños but others will share more widely in building and living under a more equitable social order.

The field research for this book was done in 1966, but for various reasons we finished the manuscript only in 1971. For purposes of presentation, however—and because we believe that what we report has lost little of its accuracy and none of its relevance since 1966—we have often used the present tense on the pages that follow. The historical present also serves as a reminder that by the time we left Jalapa it had become much more than a mere research site. For us, it was by then a familiar pattern of streets, buildings, sounds, sights, and smells, a community and a society with specific charms and problems, the home of people we were privileged to call friends.

Among those who helped us we particularly want to thank Professor Roberto Bravo Garzón, Director of the Facultad de Economía, and his staff at the Universidad Veracruzana, who generously offered invaluable aid and encouragement. José Luís Montero, Francisco Barrera Rendón, and the late Ingeniero Jacobo Ortega were valued friends and informants. Sr. Carlos Lascurain and his family and Sra. Guadalupe Remes and her family were constant sources of friendship and support, contributing greatly to the pleasure of life in Jalapa. Many other Jalapeños assisted us by providing the information on which this study is based. Most, cloaked in the anonymity of our citizen survey, are not personally known to us. Dozens of others with whom we spent long hours in discussion and whom we thus remember vividly must also remain anonymous as part of the bargain struck with informants. To all of these unnamed but helpful Jalapeños we offer our thanks.

In Mexico City, El Colegio de México provided a congenial academic home away from home, and Mario Ojeda and Rafael Segovia offered wise advice. Judy Peterson, Patricia Stea, and Sharon McKenna were also all helpful in numerous ways. In California, Henry Dietz, Ann Rice, and Don Roberts wrestled with data and the computer. Gabriel Almond, J. G. Bell, Nobu Ike, and Autumn Stanley all read and worked on the manuscript, struggling to exorcise confused ideas, faulty interpretations, disorganized chapters, and clumsy prose. Finally, for the past two years Barbara Stallings has been endlessly supportive

as data analyst, critic, and friend. Her mark is on this book in
many ways.

The number of committees, boards, foundations, and institutions to which one can become indebted for both financial and
moral support in a few short years is astounding. At one time
or another in doing our research and writing we received financial support from the Foreign Area Training Fellowship program of the Ford Foundation, the Davis campus of the University of California, and—at Stanford—Latin American Studies,
Political Studies, and International Studies. As it has done for
scores of others, the Center for Advanced Study in the Be-
havioral Sciences provided facilities for writing and reflection.
Much of the typing and computational work for this book were
done by the Center's cheerful and efficient staff.

Finally, Leonardo Vadillo Paulsen ("Vadillo") and Eduardo
del Rio ("Rius") were extremely generous in contributing their
cartoons. Those by Vadillo were first published in the Mexican
magazine *Siempre!* in the years 1966–69; they appear on our
pages 25, 46, 92, 105, 114, 159, and 170. The cartoons by Rius
come from the now discontinued magazine *Política*, 1966–67;
they appear on our pages 37, 58, and 130.

Contents

Tables

Politics and Privilege
in a Mexican City

For unto everyone that hath shall be given, and he shall have abundance: but from him that hath not shall be taken away even that which he hath.

MATTHEW 25:29

One
Introduction

The trip from Mexico City to Jalapa, capital of the state of Veracruz, is best made by highway. The roads are excellent and the journey takes only four hours. The more direct of the two routes —about 190 miles—leaves Mexico City to the northeast by superhighway, soon turning eastward onto a two-lane road past the pyramids of Teotihuacán. The next two hours spent crossing the state of Tlaxcala give the traveler some feeling for the old agricultural area of central Mexico, a high arid plateau studded with mountains and snow-capped volcanic peaks. Slightly over an hour short of Jalapa this route joins the alternate one that left Mexico City in a more southeasterly direction, winding through the state of Puebla, past an ever-growing array of factories. The two roads to Jalapa, one through peasant farming areas in Tlaxcala and the other past the Volkswagen plant in Puebla, thus symbolize many of the contrasts of Mexico today: tradition and modernity, agriculture and industry.

Shortly after the two routes meet, the highway begins its abrupt descent to the Gulf of Mexico and the port city of Veracruz almost 8,000 feet below. The deserts and arid fields of the high country give way to the greenery and lush vegetation of the subtropics. Soon thereafter Jalapa becomes visible in the distance, built astride numerous hills not quite a mile above sea level. To the southwest looms Mexico's highest mountain, the snow-capped extinct volcano Citlaltépetl; to the east lies the Gulf of Mexico.

Except for two striking architectural complexes at the western edge of the city—the Museum of Anthropology and the Normal School—Jalapa at first looks much like many other Mexican cities, with its one- and two-story adobe brick or concrete houses strung along narrow, sometimes unpaved streets. But it also differs from cities on the central plateau, particularly in the richness of the subtropical flora softening its urban landscape. Furthermore, Veracruz is a coastal state, tied more intimately to the Gulf and Caribbean cultures and less intimately to the Indian heritage of the plateau than are communities in central Mexico. Thus, Jalapa has strong cultural as well as geographical links to the coast. There is a certain gregariousness and openness to the city; carnival flourishes.[1] Marimba sounds are common among the street bands, and the traditional Veracruz harp is used, an instrument much less frequently heard in music from the highlands. Farmers and other fieldworkers (*campesinos*) coming to the city to shop, trade, or deal with the bureaucracy often wear the coastal garb of white shirt and pants. This dress is less common at greater distances from the coast, where the campesinos more often wear serapes or ponchos, darker and heavier clothing more suitable to the colder weather at higher elevations. Neither the coast nor the plateau has fully triumphed in Jalapa; a visitor who tarries more than a few days is soon exposed to elements of both cultures.

An Introduction to the Community

Although Jalapa was not in the core area of any of the great pre-Columbian civilizations, it was once well populated with Huastecas and a variety of Olmec and Toltec peoples.[2] As the Aztec

[1] In his expressive short novel *La comparsa* (Mexico: Editorial Joaquín Mortiz, 1964), Sergio Galindo has succeeded well in capturing the *ambiente* and cultural meaning of carnival in Jalapa.

[2] The historical materials at the beginning of this section are taken from Francisco González de Cossío, *Xalapa, breve reseña histórica* (Mexico: Talleres Gráficos de la Nación, 1957). This is the traditional spelling of the city's name, but the modern Jalapa is more frequently used. See also José Luis Melgarejo V., *Breve historia de Veracruz* (Jalapa: Universidad Veracruzana, 1960).

empire expanded toward the coast it established an uneasy and shifting domain over the area. The region was never completely pacified, however, and continuing rebellions shook the hold of the center on the fertile valleys.

Cortés and his men passed through Jalapa in 1519, having intentionally chosen to approach Mexico City through Tlaxcala and pueblos hostile to the Aztecs. A decision based on military considerations became a pattern reinforced by other flows of men and goods. Jalapa became a significant stopping place on the road that led from Veracruz to Mexico City, increasing in size and importance through the colonial period. Because of its natural beauty and agreeable climate, a number of Spanish families built homes in Jalapa to which they came when the lowland heat of Veracruz became oppressive. By the end of the sixteenth century, Jalapa contained a modest array of administrative offices, a Franciscan monastery, and a hospital, as well as the growing community of permanent and semipermanent residents.

By the seventeenth century the area had become important for its commercial sugar plantations, and slaves were brought in to supplement the diminishing Indian labor supply. At the same time, the Spanish population increased, owing in part to the constant threat of piracy in the port city of Veracruz. Goods meant for exportation came to be stored in the more secure warehouses of Jalapa, and families and commercial enterprises moved to the city as a result. From about 1720 on, this commercial activity was intensified as annual fairs displaying the wares of Spain and her colonies became a major feature of Jalapeño life, attracting buyers and merchants from many inland areas. Fifty years later, however, this expansionist era came to an abrupt close with the reforms of Charles III. Free trade was introduced, the fairs were ended, and the nascent tobacco industry was badly damaged by the establishment of a crown monopoly. Once again Veracruz's commercial ascendancy was established, and Jalapa returned to a primarily agricultural way of life.

The economic problems of the city were further exacerbated

during the Independence period when Jalapa was under constant pressure to provide quarters and supplies for Spanish soldiers sent to defend the Crown. Hidalgo rebels damaged the town in 1811, and subsequently local Indians joined the revolt, isolating the city from Veracruz. Within a year the roads were once again open, but further economic damage had already been done. As order was restored after Independence, Jalapa was named administrative capital of the state of Veracruz. Except for a brief interval from 1878 to 1885, it has remained the state capital, but never again did its economy boom as in the seventeenth and early eighteenth centuries.

It might be noted that it was not only the Spaniards and, subsequently, the French troops of Maximilian who marched through the city. In 1847, American troops under the command of General Winfield Scott invaded Jalapa, and some remained quartered there until the ratification of the treaty of Guadalupe Hidalgo in 1848. It was unfortunate but perhaps in a way appropriate that Jalapa suffered in these campaigns against Antonio López de Santa Anna, for the antic caudillo was in fact born and reared in the city, its most famous if hardly its most admired native son.[3]

The Porfiriato, the Revolution, and the recovery of the 1940's all affected the city, although it never occupied center stage.[4] A modest commercial recovery was coupled with the growth of the coffee and tobacco industries, and the bureaucratic and governmental sectors of the city's economy burgeoned as centralism

[3] Santa Anna's troops were defeated in 1847 by the Americans in Cerro Gordo, about 15 miles outside Jalapa. A number of future Civil War generals fought in Scott's forces, including both Lee and Grant.

[4] See Mario Gill, "Veracruz: revolución y extremismo," *Historia Mexicana*, 2.4 (April–June, 1954): 618–36. Gill, writing fom a Marxist perspective, argues that the state of Veracruz was a center of popular protest during the 1920's. Nevertheless, the state was not important in the Mexican Revolution, and the city of Veracruz saw more political clashes and nascent mass movements than Jalapa. See also the eye-witness reportage on politics in Jalapa and Veracruz in Maurice Halperin, "Inside Mexico," *Current History*, 45.5 (Feb. 1937): 83–87. For more detail, see John B. Williman, "Church and State in Veracruz, 1840–1940" (unpublished doctoral dissertation, St. Louis University, 1971).

and the Mexican version of big government became realities. But the basic features of city life and the prospects for Jalapa's future in the second half of the twentieth century remained essentially unchanged.

If Jalapa has never suffered the sharp economic reversals experienced by Mexican cities that were inordinately dependent on mining or on a single crop, neither has it benefited greatly from Mexico's postwar "economic miracle." Its industrial sector is relatively small, which means that employment opportunities are limited. The growth and stability that have been achieved depend on its position as an administrative, commercial, educational, and marketing center for the region. The state government—including the state university—is the largest single employer, and additional government jobs are to be found in the approximately 25 federal agencies maintaining local offices, and in the *ayuntamiento* (municipal government).[5] This predominance of officialdom leads many citizens to refer to Jalapa as a bureaucratic community.

Second only to Jalapa's dependence on government is its dependence on coffee. Although only a relatively small quantity is grown in the *municipio* itself, the city is the major processing and marketing center for Veracruz's extensive coffee-growing region. In nearby rural areas, many small private farms and *ejidos* (communally owned farms) grow beans and sell them to processors in Jalapa. The five major and several smaller processing plants situated in the city clean, sort, roast, and then sell both to the national and to the all-important international market.

Although the processing industry itself now provides fewer jobs than it did prior to mechanization, it still has a major economic impact. The city is the primary commercial center for a large rural population whose economic well-being is intimately tied to the level of coffee production, the available coffee markets, and the market price. Furthermore, Jalapa is the home of

[5] The count of 25 is based on listings in the 1966 telephone book. Although listings are notoriously incomplete and phone service is limited, it was assumed that federal officers would in fact have telephones and be listed.

a number of very wealthy families whose fortunes derive largely from coffee processing and exporting. These families not only dominate the local coffee industry, but have expanded their holdings to include many of the community's largest commercial establishments, smaller industries, and important blocks of real estate. Their pre-eminent political and economic concern is the international coffee market, and specifically the prices and sales quotas allocated to Mexico and the Jalapa region. Of the ten members of the local coffee exporters' association in 1966, six or seven were among the "biggest men" in the community's private economy.

A casual visitor might be surprised to hear of the importance of coffee processing in Jalapa, for the plants are inconspicuously situated and not physically impressive. More evident are the regional distribution facility of the government-owned petroleum industry (PEMEX), a factory making laminated wood products, and a textile factory. In 1966, only the last employed any sizeable number of people (about 300), and its economic position was by no means secure. Outdated equipment and unfavorable market conditions have already forced two major textile factories out of business in Jalapa, and the remaining one faces continuing questions of mechanization and profitability. The empty railroad repair shops stand as another reminder of technological change and declining activity. Jalapa is located on one of the two main rail links between the port of Veracruz and the industrialized regions of the interior. In the days of more primitive equipment and slower operations, the shops were busy and prosperous. They have long been closed, however, joining the textile mills as relics of another age.

Jalapa today is the second largest city in the state, exceeded in population by the port of Veracruz, situated about 75 miles to the southeast. At the time of our study, Jalapa had about 95,000 inhabitants. The considerable growth of recent decades (see Table 1.1) is evident in the relatively undeveloped condition of many public facilities and the appearance of new housing on the city's outskirts. Most of the people (about 85,000) live in the

TABLE 1.1

Population of Jalapa, 1930–66

Year	Total	Urban only (city)
1930	40,250	36,810
1940	46,830	39,530
1950	59,280	51,170
1960	78,120	69,440
1966	95,000	85,000

SOURCE: Figures for 1930–60 come from Secretaría de Industria y Comercio, Dirección General de Estadística, *VIII Censo General de Población, 1960; Tomo I: Estado de Veracruz* (México, D.F., 1964), Cuadro 1, p. 41. Figures for 1966 are calculated from an official estimate of 3.4 percent as the mean annual growth for the 1961–66 period, using the 1960 census data as a base. Results are rounded to the nearest thousand.

urban section of the municipio (legally there is no such entity as a city in Mexico), with only another 10,000 scattered in the surrounding farms and hamlets. Jalapa is thus overwhelmingly urban in residence and style of life.

Although there was substantial population growth during the 1960's, the municipio has not been flooded with desperately poor rural dwellers as have some other urban centers in Mexico. Perhaps a quarter of the population migrated to the city between 1955 and 1966. Although caution must be used in interpreting our survey data, these relatively recent arrivals do not seem to differ significantly from their more rooted neighbors in their distribution in the lowest income groups or the manual occupations.[6] In short, our impression was that Jalapa has attracted a

[6] Because of incomplete census maps, our survey undersampled the newest and poorest settlements. The estimates here—and all data presented on the adult population of Jalapa unless otherwise noted—are derived from interviews of 399 adults. The stratified sample constituted by these 399 adults intentionally overrepresented the upper class by a factor of three (because the upper-class N would otherwise have been too small) and unintentionally overrepresented women (because they were more frequently at home). Faced with the necessity of weighting the sample to represent the class and sex distribution of the entire population, we inflated the N's of underrepresented groups rather than reducing the N's of overrepresented groups, creating an ultimate analytical sample N of 1,556. See Appendix B for an English translation of the questionnaire used and Appendix C for further details on sampling, weighting, and other methodological concerns.

rather mixed group of recent arrivals who, although they have contributed substantially to pressures on urban services and jobs, have not added a massive squatter or slum dimension to the municipio.

The urban populace lives in single-family homes and, to a lesser extent, in small apartment buildings. Although there are exceptions, the residences of the poor tend to be situated on the periphery of the city, thus forming roughly concentric rings of impoverishment around a more privileged core. The generally narrow streets are filled with activity during the daytime, except from about one to four P.M. as residents take the midday break. Normal business hours run from nine or ten in the morning to about one in the afternoon, and from about four in the afternoon through eight or nine in the evening. The few main thorough-fares are full of traffic and noisy with the unmuffled exhausts of the ubiquitous Servicio Urbano buses. These main streets are well paved and except for the volume of traffic and the limited number of lanes (usually two) are easily traveled. Other, more residential, streets are paved sometimes with concrete or asphalt but more often with paving stones. Although carefully built and normally bordered by raised sidewalks, these streets must be driven slowly and carefully. As distances from the city's center grow, these secondary streets usually deteriorate into unpaved roads without sidewalks.

Social, political, and commercial activities are concentrated in a section of the city informally called *el centro*. There, in a rela-tively small area, are found government offices, numerous stores, restaurants, hotels and office buildings (including modern struc-tures of steel, concrete, and glass that are six to eight stories high), the city's four movie houses, and the army barracks. There too is the political and symbolic center of Jalapa, the state capi-tal building. It faces the main cathedral, the city hall (*palacio municipal*), some large office buildings, and a park dedicated to Benito Juárez. The park looks to the southeast over the lowest section of the city and two prominent landmarks, the federal

Social Security Hospital and the new campus of the Universidad Veracruzana.[7]

As we shall have ample opportunity to suggest, the physical aspects of the city—centralized, orderly; a core of modernity surrounded by substantial impoverishment—can stand as an introductory metaphor for its political life. Politics too is centralized, quite orderly, and organized around an active core of *políticos*, bureaucrats, and a minority of citizens. But more than metaphor is needed in order to come to grips with politics in Jalapa. Thus, we now turn to the analytical and intellectual underpinnings of the study that follows.

The Study of Community Politics

Despite immodest claims to the contrary, any approach to the study of a political system is always partial and thus inevitably prejudiced. One student grabs the trunk of the beast, another embraces the leg, a third fondles the ear, a fourth touches the tail, a fifth collides with the torso. Motivations and purposes also differ. Some students are simply stumbling through the swamp when they encounter leviathan; others are hunters in search of trophies; some lead safaris of eager neophytes; others are diligent taxonomists intent on strengthening their collections; not a few are zealous patriots claiming to bring the benefits of civilization to their prey.

One responsibility of scholarship in such an imperfect world is to specify as clearly as possible in each instance why the beast is being hunted, how it is being conceptualized, and what part the scholar has hold of. In the remainder of this chapter we shall attempt to meet this responsibility as directly and briefly as possible.

[7] By 1966 the *facultades* (schools and departments) of Law, Commerce, and Architecture as well as the main library, a university-run preparatory school, and the stadium, were located on the new campus. The facultad of Economics and the School of Pedagogy, Philosophy, and Letters were still in the central city. Other university facilities are located in the cities of Veracruz and Orizaba.

The most obvious characteristic of our study is that it involves a single subnational case. That is, we have chosen to explore certain characteristics of Mexican politics by examining the political life of a single city in detail. We thus locate ourselves within a well established, if not uncontroversial, set of approaches to the study of social and political phenomena—the genre known loosely as community political studies.

The theory, methodology, and substantive findings of community studies have been the subject of an avalanche of analysis and polemic, and we have no intention of entering into this seemingly endless and sometimes sterile debate. On the other hand, our study cannot be wholly divorced from the controversies and critical problems that this literature raises. Thus, we have organized the discussion that follows around two quite general questions: What aspects of Mexican politics (and by extension what aspects of politics in general) do we hope to illuminate with this case? What are some of the advantages and disadvantages of approaching these topics through a study of Jalapa? The first question directs attention to the focus and purposes of the research and the second to its generalizability and representativeness.

The key intellectual challenge in the analysis of Mexican politics lies not in the description of decisional participation—"who governs?"—but rather in the explication of the sources and consequences of the entire process of governance.[8] By governance

[8] The phrase, which of course comes from Robert A. Dahl, *Who Governs? Democracy and Power in an American City* (Yale University Press, 1961), can be taken as shorthand for an approach to the study of community politics that emphasizes process and participation in the making of local decisions. It is our view that this is not the most fruitful approach to an understanding of Mexican politics. Much the same view is expressed regarding Latin American communities in general by Francine F. Rabinovitz in "Sound and Fury Signifying Nothing? A Review of Community Power Research in Latin America," *Urban Affairs Quarterly*, 3.3 (March 1968): 111–22 (see particularly her final three pages entitled "Who Cares Who Governs?"), and regarding third-world cities in general by Donald B. Rosenthal, "Functions of Urban Political Systems: Comparative Analysis and the Indian Case," in Terry N. Clark, ed., *Community Structure and Decision-Making: Comparative Analyses* (San Francisco, 1968).

is meant much more than authoritative decision-making. Included are such topics as the construction, linkage, and maintenance of authority structures, the interactions between these structures and ordinary as well as not-so-ordinary citizens, and the distribution of advantage and disadvantage that characterizes these interactions.

Thus, the organizing framework of questions for our analysis includes the following:

How is community politics related to state and national politics?

What are the institutional ties and the major purposes and goals of those who occupy positions of political authority?

How are demands handled and outcomes shaped by the men and institutions in charge of the political business of the community? And who determines what the political business of the community shall be?

What are the social-structural bases of political institutions and participation? How do the functioning of these institutions and the flow of participation affect the distribution of opportunities and benefits?

What are the patterns observable in citizens' values, beliefs, and expectations, and how do these patterns fit with political practices in the community?

How is the process of governance maintained? What supports the political status quo and what threatens it?

This admittedly preliminary and imperfectly integrated set of questions suggests that we are not primarily interested in the study of what is commonly called community power. Of course in the analysis of subjects such as state and national influence on local politics, the manner in which the proper "political business" of the community is defined, the distribution of benefits and opportunities, and the maintenance of political stability, questions about the exercise of power will inevitably crop up.

But nowhere in the study do we set out explicitly to discover who has power over whom, to what degree, within what domains of activity, and under what circumstances.

There is, however, one approach to the study of community power that has been quite influential on our thinking about Mexico and Jalapa. This approach, emphasizing what Peter Bachrach and Morton S. Baratz have called the hidden, agenda-shaping or "second face" of power, focuses on those men, institutions, and activities that determine what comes to the center of political attention and who is benefited and advantaged by politics: "Political systems and sub-systems develop a 'mobilization of bias,' a set of predominant values, beliefs, rituals, and institutional procedures ('rules of the game') that operate systematically and consistently to the benefit of certain persons and groups at the expense of others. Those who benefit are placed in a preferred position to defend and promote their vested interests."[9] In short, this approach sensitizes us to the importance of studying the manner in which flows of public policy, rewards, and disadvantages are shaped by configurations of political structure, values, and beliefs.

It is fashionable for critics of this second-face-of-power approach to claim that it necessarily involves the identification of nondecisions—issues that never get on the decisional agenda. The empirical study of such "nonevents," the critics continue, is impossible. When the approach is so narrowly conceived, there may well be some truth in this criticism, but basically it in no way diminishes the importance or possibility of studying the manner in which political structures and the rules of the game limit and shape public policy outcomes.

A certain amount of confusion arises on this score because Bachrach, Baratz, and others who share their perspective have themselves been deeply influenced by decision-making models. Thus, they sometimes tend to see community policies, institu-

[9] This position is most fully developed in their *Power and Poverty: Theory and Practice* (Oxford University Press, 1970), here quoted from p. 43.

tions, and values as conditioned and manipulated by an elite engaged in what they call "nondecision-making." In such models, keeping certain issues out of the public arena is a primary goal and activity of the political elite, and thus a key manifestation of the second face of power: "nondecision-making is a means by which demands for change in the existing allocation of benefits and privileges in the community can be suffocated before they are even voiced; or kept covert; or killed before they gain access to the relevant decision-making arena; or, failing all these things, maimed or destroyed in the decision-implementing stage of the policy process."[10] Although simple observation suggests that such models are valid in some communities, the usefulness of the overall perspective does not depend on the demonstration of an elite engaged in nondecision-making. Quite clearly, institutions and culture also have power over the behavior of men even when it is not possible to identify a manipulative elite that suppresses demands and determines agendas. One need not subscribe to a neo-elitist model of the political process to appreciate that in many settings political recruitment and participation are systematically constricted, challenges to the status quo effectively turned aside, and citizens' problems routinely prevented from becoming matters of public concern. In fact, the development and persistence of such characteristics in the Mexican political system are subjects for research precisely because they are *not* fully explainable as the consequences of the behavior of a little band of willful men.

Jalapa as a Community and as a Case

Either explicit or implicit in many community studies is the notion that local politics in some manner reflects the norms, institutions, and behavior of the larger polity. This does not mean, of course, that the community is assumed to be a political microcosm of the nation. Quite the contrary, the community—because of its smaller size and more limited goals—is often thought to

---

[10] *Ibid.*, p. 44.

practice a style of politics that is impossible at the national level. Nevertheless, certain similarities in institutions, political attitudes, consensual mechanisms, or bargaining processes seem to indicate that the study of community politics can teach us something about the substance and dynamics of the larger system.[11]

Illumination of the larger system would be particularly likely where, owing to historical arrangements and to centralized decision-making and control of resources, community politics is intimately related structurally to regional and national politics— where, for example, community leaders owe their positions to, derive much of their support from, and in the final analysis have to answer to higher levels of leadership, or where important community benefits come directly from regional and national agencies. Of course some penetration of the local system by regional and national institutions occurs in almost all communities, but in certain settings the influence of higher levels of government is so pervasive and important as to constitute a defining characteristic of local politics. In such cases the value of community studies lies not only in what local political practices and norms can teach us about national politics and values, but also in the opportunity to examine the linkages between several levels of authority structures. The community may then be viewed as an arena for many political forces, only a few of which are generated locally. The notion of community politics is thus extended to include any political activity taking place in the community, whatever its origins.[12]

It is with this conception of the utility of a community study that we have approached Jalapa.

There is, however, no such thing as a fully representative Mex-

[11] For a useful statement on the case-study method and also on community studies as cases see Conrad M. Arensberg, "The Community as Object and Sample," *American Anthropologist*, 63.2 (Part I, April 1961): 241–64. For a successful and unpretentious study of a community selected to represent events in the larger system see William S. Allen, *The Nazi Seizure of Power: The Experience of a Single German Town, 1930–1935* (Chicago, 1965).

[12] See Marc J. Swartz, ed., *Local-Level Politics: Social and Cultural Perspectives* (Chicago, 1968), p. 1; and Norton E. Long, "The Local Community as an Ecology of Games," *American Journal of Sociology*, 64.3 (Nov. 1958): 251–61.

ican community. Size, level of economic development, cultural mix, regional characteristics, and a host of other factors combine to produce a rich diversity even among those communities that are clearly linked to the dominant national system. Although a huge modern city like Monterrey in the north and an overgrown village like San Cristóbal in the south are both legally *municipios* and important in their immediate regions, they differ very markedly in the ways in which they are governed and the degree to which they are tied to state and national politics.[13] The choice of a community for intensive study, therefore, could not be based on general notions of representativeness, but had to be based on limited and specific criteria. In an initial sorting of such criteria, we established the following guidelines.

(1) The community should be located in what is commonly called the "core" of Mexico, the central states that have dominated the country politically, culturally, demographically, and economically (with the exception of northern agriculture and industry).

(2) The community should be large enough and modern enough to present a full range of twentieth-century situations and problems. Its social and occupational structure should be urban and therefore relatively diverse. (Against our desire for size, modernity, and diversity had to be balanced our limited resources for research. A municipio of 50,000 to 100,000 people was thought to be appropriate.)

(3) On the continuum between severe political schism and open community conflict on the one hand and stability and successful management of conflict on the other, a community near the latter end should be favored. Politically well managed communities are the norm in Mexico; highly conflictual communities—or at least those that are publicly conflictual—are deviant cases.[14]

[13] Even within the same state, differences may be marked. See, for example, the interesting comparative study of two cities in Chiapas as reported in Jorge Capriata, "The Political Culture of Marginal Elites: A Case Study of Regionalism in Mexican Politics" (unpublished doctoral dissertation, Stanford University, 1971).

[14] The rationale for this criterion will become apparent in the following

Thus oriented, we eventually selected Jalapa, the charming subtropical city introduced at the beginning of this chapter. Of course Jalapa is not and could not possibly be considered perfectly representative of middle-sized Mexican cities. Even if Mexico's regional, economic, and cultural diversity were not so great, Jalapeño politics is special in three interrelated ways. It is well to have these in mind from the outset even though they will be elaborated in much greater detail in the chapters that follow. First, Jalapa is a state capital. The most obvious and important consequence of this fact is that there is an inordinate degree of higher governmental presence in local politics. Municipal government, traditionally subordinate to state politics throughout Mexico, is even more thoroughly subjugated than usual in Jalapa. Without question, the governor is the most important political personage in the city, and his real or anticipated actions and reactions dominate local politics. This is not to say that the governor constantly intervenes in local affairs, but he lives in the city, and no politically active person forgets it for very long.

Second, Jalapa is an unusually well managed municipio, characterized by public order, stability, domination of political life by the official party (the Partido Revolucionario Institucional, or PRI), and cooperation with—or apathy toward—public officials on the part of the citizens. From the point of view of the government/Party apparatus, Jalapa is a "good town." There is minimal political conflict, almost no formal opposition, and little overt discontent; even the university has not been so "troublesome" as some other provincial universities. If the top chieftains in the government/Party apparatus were to offer awards in good management to regional and local *políticos*, those who govern Jalapa would undoubtedly receive one of them.

---

chapter, where a model of relevant aspects of Mexican politics is presented. Also, we were influenced by knowledge that a study of a more openly conflictual and politically heterogeneous Mexican community was soon to be undertaken. This study is reported in Antonio Ugalde, *Power and Conflict in a Mexican Community* (University of New Mexico Press, 1970). In the final selection of Jalapa, logistics (proximity to Mexico City), personal contacts, and expectations about access to officials and to records were also important.

Finally, as nearly as can be determined, the occupational, educational, and income levels of the city are somewhat above average for urban Mexico.[15] Together, the University and the numerous government offices attract an atypically large number of relatively well educated persons to Jalapa. The city can boast of its own symphony orchestra and enjoys frequent visits by professional opera, dance, and theater companies. There are also public lectures by experts in many fields, and the usual local literary and cultural events. By no means prosperous or booming, Jalapa nevertheless enjoys substantial economic security by virtue of the essential governmental, commercial, and educational services it supplies. The style of local politics is both cause and consequence of this situation of security-without-prosperity.

Relatively advantaged, well managed, secure, and insulated from change and conflict, Jalapa is outwardly an untroubled city. This could be said of dozens of other Mexican cities, but the degree of good management and public harmony found in Jalapa is somewhat exceptional, something of an exaggeration. The hand of the state is heavier, opposition parties are weaker, citizens are better satisfied, and conflict is less frequent than usual. These findings, although diminishing somewhat our capacity to generalize from Jalapa to other communities, can be turned to our advantage at many other points in the analysis. With these special characteristics in mind from the outset, we can minimize their costs and maximize their benefits as we deal first with a general overview of Mexican politics and then with a more specific description of the governance of Jalapa.

[15] For data comparing some demographic and attitudinal characteristics of the population of Jalapa with similar characteristics of the total urban population of Mexico (and with census data where appropriate) see Appendix A. Jalapeños tend (in comparison with urban Mexicans in general) to be better satisfied with their current style of life and more active politically. These findings follow quite predictably from their generally higher levels of income, education, and occupational status.

Two

Aspects of the Mexican Political System

This chapter is not a general and exhaustive model of Mexican politics. Rather, it is a series of connected propositions about those aspects of the Mexican political system that are most relevant to an understanding of politics in Jalapa. For example, although the political economy of Mexico is deeply intertwined with that of the United States in ways that influence decision-making at the national level, these factors are of limited importance in the politics of Jalapa. Thus, they are not discussed below.

Also, there will not be any section specifically devoted to mechanisms of political control. It has become popular in certain circles to view the Mexican political system as a set of institutions and practices for the control of the population in general and oppositionist groups in particular. When the standard practices of control break down—as in the summer of 1968—violent repression may be used. This emphasis on control and repression is a needed corrective to various celebrations of "democratic" Mexico; but what is impressive about the politics of Jalapa is the manner in which both the behavior of ordinary citizens and the behavior of elites are shaped so as to *obviate* the formal and public exercise of political controls. In the city one does not sense, nor do the data to be presented suggest, that repressive controls are much used, threatened, or feared. Thus we concentrate on informal and structural controls, on the manner in which norms, institutions, and custom coalesce to support a form of politics-as-normal in which conflict is muted, opposition is absorbed, and political failure is in part defined as the necessity of actually using the impressive state apparatus of public control and repression.[1]

Finally, it should be noted that the model is not independent of the data gathered in Jalapa. In deciding what roles to emphasize, what structures and processes are more rather than less important, and how the system fits together, we have been deeply influenced by what we found there. This, of course, does not mean that the data, analyses, inferences, and conclusions of the study are all implied in the model. On the contrary, much of what is sketched on the following pages will become meaningful only when supported by data and analyzed in terms of the political realities of Jalapa.

Centralization and Hierarchy

In 1965 Licenciado Carlos Madrazo, as president of the National Executive Committee of the PRI, experimented with holding primaries within the Party. There was some speculation at the time that this partial "democratization" of the Party's operation was being tried without the wholehearted approval of Presi-

---

[1] We have found the following articles and books particularly useful: Bo Anderson and James D. Cockcroft, "Control and Cooptation in Mexican Politics," *International Journal of Comparative Sociology*, 7.1 (March 1966): 2–28; Frank R. Brandenburg, *The Making of Modern Mexico* (Englewood Cliffs, N.J., 1964); Howard F. Cline, *Mexico: Revolution to Evolution, 1940–1960* (New York, 1963); William P. Glade, Jr., and Charles W. Anderson, *The Political Economy of Mexico* (University of Wisconsin Press, 1963); Pablo González Casanova, *La Democracia en México*, 2nd ed. (Mexico, D.F.: Ediciones ERA, 1967); Vincent L. Padgett, *The Mexican Political System* (Boston, 1966); Robert E. Scott, *Mexican Government in Transition*, 2nd ed. (University of Illinois Press, 1964), and "Mexico: The Established Revolution," in Lucian W. Pye and Sidney Verba, eds., *Political Culture and Political Development* (Princeton University Press, 1965); Raymond Vernon, *The Dilemma of Mexico's Development* (Harvard University Press, 1963); James W. Wilkie, *The Mexican Revolution: Federal Expenditure and Social Change Since 1910* (University of California Press, 1967). See also Roger D. Hansen, *The Politics of Mexican Development* (The Johns Hopkins Press, 1971), and Kenneth F. Johnson, *Mexican Democracy: A Critical View* (Boston, 1971).

dent Gustavo Díaz Ordaz. As a highly placed Mexican friend put it, however, "Sr. Madrazo has a political life expectancy of approximately 45 seconds if he should really displease the President. It is that long only because our telephone service is bad." Indeed, when the democratization experiments failed, Madrazo was removed from his post, assumed a marginally oppositionist role in politics, and was subsequently killed along with many others in a commercial air disaster (which his friends and admirers suggested was the result of sabotage).

It is not necessary, however, to rely on such oft-told tales, whether documented or apocryphal, to support the proposition that the Mexican political apparatus is centralized and hierarchical. Students of modern Mexico are in substantial agreement that a presidentially centered coalition, operating through both the PRI and the governmental bureaucracies, sets the main directions of public policy, regulates a vast system of recruitment and patronage, and adjudicates the conflicts and strains that arise in the conduct of ordinary and extraordinary political and public business.[2] Among other things, the President and his circle set national priorities, mediate conflicting claims on public resources, allocate men and money, select and elevate to office all state governors, many municipal presidents, and thousands of other candidates and officials, and manage and manipulate the symbolic capital of the Mexican Revolution—all with minimal reference to either the legislative or the judicial branch of government, and probably with fewer constraints imposed by the PRI members and the bureaucracy than generally imagined.

In such a system, each successive level of government is weaker, more dependent, and more impoverished than the level above. Since the municipality is at the bottom of the federal-state-local chain, it is in reality—despite its official designation

---

[2] The best description of this system is Brandenburg, especially Chapter 1, "The Revolutionary Family and the Mexican Proposition," and Chapter 6, "The Liberal Machiavellian." A survey of different views on where power is located is offered in Carolyn and Martin Needleman, "Who Rules Mexico? A Critique of Some Current Views on the Mexican Political Process," *Journal of Politics*, 31.4 (Nov. 1969): 1011–34.

as the *municipio libre* (free municipality)—the least autonomous unit of government in the republic. An ayuntamiento or municipal government is normally constituted at the pleasure of the state authorities, is in control of very few funds, and is limited juridically and politically to caretaker and administrative functions.[3] Of course a great many particularistic factors affect the degree and severity of control exercised over a specific municipal government. For example, when the state governor enjoys close relationships with the federal executive, his capacity for intervening in municipio affairs is probably enhanced; where local commercial and industrial elites are important and not completely captured by the government and Party apparatuses, the exercise of centralized control over community politics is rendered more difficult and the outcomes more problematical. But no such qualifications should be allowed to detract from the general proposition that the resources, opportunities, and decisional latitude available at the local level are everywhere in Mexico sharply diminished through the mechanisms of executive centralism.[4]

This has been the case since the beginning of the twentieth century, but improvements in transportation, communication, and the organizational capacity of government and Party bureaucracies have increased the relative deprivation of the municipios over recent decades. This trend is easiest to document

[3] The juridical basis of centralization in Mexico is very important. The ayuntamiento is closely regulated by state laws, which even go so far as to specify many of its administrative procedures. Financial supervision is particularly close. In Veracruz, annual ayuntamiento budgets must be approved in advance by the state government, transactions must be reported monthly, and all revenue sources are closely regulated. Article 12 of the state constitution of Veracruz states: "No one is obligated to pay any tax not previously authorized by either the national or the state government. Ayuntamientos can assess fees only on those areas of activity legally designated as acceptable sources of municipal revenues, permission being given in the form of approval by the state legislature." Ostensibly designed to protect citizens from exploitation by local government, such legislation actually operates to insure control of the municipio by state and national authorities.

[4] For a supporting case study see Lawrence S. Graham, *Politics in a Mexican Community*, University of Florida Monographs, no. 35 (University of Florida Press, 1968), particularly Chapters 3 and 5 and the Concluding Remarks.

in fiscal affairs, where the local share of government income has dropped steadily from 8.9 percent of the national total in 1932 to 2.6 percent in 1960, but it is also evident in non-fiscal transactions and distributions.[5]

Thus, as Mexico has become more modern and more highly developed in the socioeconomic sense, the political center has increasingly monopolized critical decisions. Regional strong men, independent labor and peasant leaders, and politically non-integrated economic elites are probably rarer than they were a few decades ago. As the scope of government activity has widened and as political and regulative penetration of society has increased, centralization has proceeded apace. Thus, although government is more important than ever before in the daily life of the people, the policies of that government are increasingly being made in decisional centers far removed from their experience and reach. This phenomenon is not, of course, particular to Mexico. It is, however, especially acute there. Even a routine (although important) decision concerning electrification or drainage in the municipio will often be out of the hands of local authorities and located, for political or economic reasons, in some state or federal office less sensitive to community needs and more insulated from local pressures.

Hierarchical differences have other consequences. Authorities at one level are disadvantaged in countless ways when dealing with authorities at higher levels. Bargaining in the hierarchy is sharply skewed in favor of those on top. As stated very bluntly by a governor of the state of Baja California when he turned down a request for funds from the municipio of Ensenada, "A mi me chinga el gobierno federal, y yo le chingo al municipal" (The federal government screws me, and I screw the municipality).[6]

[5] Wilkie, p. 3; and González Casanova, Chapter 1, section 6.

[6] As cited in Antonio Ugalde, "Conflict and Consensus in a Mexican City: A Study in Political Integration" (unpublished doctoral dissertation, Stanford University, 1968), p. 165. A much revised version of this dissertation was published as *Power and Conflict in a Mexican Community* (University of New Mexico Press, 1970), cited in Chapter 1. Much of the detail of the dissertation, including the remark quoted here, is omitted from the published version.

So unequal, for example, are the relative power positions of municipio and state that it is probable that state governments are actually disinvesting the municipios, taking in through taxes and other fees substantially more than is returned in goods and services. The surplus is invested in patronage and in public programs that frequently bear little relationship—if they are not antithetical—to local needs. Another consequence of the relative weakness of the municipio is that those with the necessary connections, experience, and other resources try to bypass local authorities when in quest of some benefit or opportunity. Even when local authorities have the nominal power to respond, their response is subject to review further up the hierarchy if the matter is of any importance outside the formal boundaries of the local system. Thus, both efficiency and security argue that it is wise to seek support and decisions as close to the center as possible lest time be wasted with those who don't count and whose decisions may subsequently be overturned. As will be elaborated in greater detail below, bargaining in this context gives certain individuals, groups, and strata great advantages at the expense of others.[7]

Leaders, Followers, and Careers

It is misleading to think of politics in Mexico as noncompetitive. Of course the opposition offered the PRI in most elections is token. Within the governmental and Party organizations, however, there exists a complex and meaningful struggle for position and advantage, as well as for the symbolic and material rewards of office. This internal competition has little to do with democracy, nor does it normally give disadvantaged groups and individuals a chance to affect the policy-making process. On the contrary, the Mexican way of handling recruitment into politics and of distributing rewards frequently contributes to the political impotence of large sectors of the population. Furthermore,

[7] A useful brief analysis of these and other consequences of Mexican political organization can be found in Rodolfo Stavenhagen, "Un modelo para el estudio de las Organizaciones Políticas en México," *Revista Mexicana de Sociología*, 29.2 (April–June 1967): 329–36.

under the prevailing rules of the career game, politicians and bureaucrats often find that personal advancement and the public interest sharply conflict. Of special interest here as most relevant to Jalapa are the situational constraints and rules of the game that shape behavior and competition at the middle and lower levels of the government and the PRI. Much of what follows, however, would apply with modifications to those higher up the hierarchy, to Brandenburg's "inner council" and "second level of the Revolutionary Family" as well as to Scott's "ruling class."[8] Although most people at these lower levels do not qualify as politically powerful (except in certain transactions with those of lower status), they are absolutely essential to the ongoing governance of Mexico and to the maintenance of the centralized system of which they form a part.

The larger context in which leader-follower relationships and political careers must be understood is the rhythm of six-year rotation of state and national administrations punctuated by a three-year cycle in ayuntamientos. At all levels there is a constitutionally prescribed complete turnover of elected officeholders under the slogan "Effective suffrage, no re-election." There is also a relatively rapid and continuous movement through appointive governmental and Party posts.[9] The norm of no re-election encourages those who aspire to public careers to move into bureaucratic and party positions while awaiting opportuni-

---

[8] Cf. Brandenburg's third level of the Revolutionary Family hierarchy (Brandenburg, pp. 2–7) and Scott's governing and mediatory classes (Scott, pp. 378–84). See also C. E. Grimes and Charles E. P. Simmons, "Bureaucracy and Political Control in Mexico: Towards an Assessment," *Public Administration Review*, 29.1, Jan.–Feb. 1969): 72–79.

[9] For example, in Ensenada from 1953 to 1967, 56 percent of the high officers of state agencies and 62 percent of the high officers of federal agencies spent two years or less in their appointed posts (Ugalde, *Conflict and Consensus*, p. 199). Moreover, of 44 officers of the PRI Municipal Committee, 24 had held a high position in the municipal bureaucracy, three had served in similar positions at the state level, and four had served at the federal level. Most of the 13 who had held no such positions expected to hold them in the future (*ibid.*, p. 207). John Womack suggests that to capture the intent of *Sufragio efectivo y no re-elección* it should be translated as "A real vote and no boss rule." See Womack, *Zapata and the Mexican Revolution* (New York, 1969), p. 55.

In search of a winner. Bones are a traditional symbol for candidates or factions in Mexican politics.

ties to run for office again; the distinction between elective and appointive office, however, is blurred because being appointed (nominated) as a PRI candidate is tantamount to being elected. More to the point, the system of relatively rapid turnover in office reminds both aspirants and incumbents that their careers are tentative and fragile, subject to being downgraded or terminated if they violate the rules of the game.

One key to understanding the sources and consequences of the fragility of officeholding is the nature of sponsorship within the apparatus. Securing a continuous and increasingly important series of posts in the government/Party apparatus—or getting back into such posts from private life—depends in large part not only on having an influential sponsor at any given moment, but also on having a variety of contingency plans should the sponsor fall from favor. To be too closely identified with an individual or faction in eclipse can end one's career. Yet since careers are built out of a sequence of appointments largely dependent on personalistic loyalties and attachments, an aggressive and successful politician often assembles a coterie of followers (*brazos*) indebted to him as chief (*jefe* or *patrón*) and necessarily identified with him. Such groupings are commonly known as *camarillas*. At all levels there is thus substantial tension between the need to be identified with and protected by a patrón, and the need to maintain sufficient independence of action, identification, and other contacts to rescue oneself should the patrón's career and influence begin to decline. When this tension is set in the context of the lack of other public opportunities, the scarcity of attractive private opportunities, and the overabundance of political aspirants, its personal and political consequences can be appreciated.

The Performance of Individuals and Administrations

The system just described encourages certain postures in public office, notably conservatism and detachment from the substance of public policy. Conservatism here means that at moments of uncertainty, incumbents and aspirants tend to respond in ways dictated by the high value placed on maintaining the system and the status quo. Detachment from the substance of public policy means that decisions are made and resources—which are meager anyway—are allocated more as political and personal forces dictate than as developmental or social criteria would demand.

As the history of modern Mexico attests, civic order and political stability have been dearly bought and are consequently highly valued by elites and ordinary citizens alike. The centralized and hierarchically organized Mexican political regime is not simply the construct of authoritarian and self-interested men; it is also the product of decades of search and experimentation by *políticos* very much concerned with ending divisive and destructive social conflict. But this perspective on the origins of the regime is not at all incompatible with a more limited perspective that views it as now strongly reinforcing conservative patterns of official behavior.

Officials are evaluated by their superiors according to their capacity to accomplish the tasks handed down from above as well as to manage the not inconsiderable challenges thrown up to them from below in the course of dealing with various clienteles. But these challenges must be handled in a special way—with absolutely minimal public controversy, disturbance, or scandal. The "good" politician or administrator is thus above all a manager of hierarchically delegated responsibilities and a manipulator of the public environment, not a responsible or responsive public servant. He serves his jefe and contributes to the latter's career not only in personalistic and private ways, but also by not letting potentially embarrassing political situations get out of hand. All of this must be done without resort to violence, overt coercion, or the most vulgar forms of corruption.[10] He is rewarded not for his innovativeness, initiative, or positive accomplishments in the making or implementing of public policy, but rather for his capacity to facilitate the functioning of the apparatus through the balancing of interests, the distribution of benefits, and the control of potentially disruptive or disequilibrating forces. When events force upon him some choice between public and personalistic service, he resorts to the trusted and well rewarded paths of narrowed public participation, continuance of practices already proved uncontroversial, and loyalty to the jefe. Conformity and conservatism are the inevitable consequences.[11]

Detachment from the substance of public policy flows naturally from the circumstances just described. In the first place, it is quite natural for bureaucrats and politicians to avoid profound involvement in or even firm stands on the substance of public policies. Except for agreement with the most general goals of national development—economic growth, mexicaniza-

[10] Violence against ordinary citizens is seldom used in urban Mexican public life, despite the events of the summers of 1968 and 1971. Much more frequent—and less visible and less condemned in the norm structure of centralized politics—is the kind of violence practiced by strong men on their opponents and on low-status dissident groups, particularly in rural areas. (We do not refer here to treatment of individuals by the police.)

[11] Compare Camilo Torres Restrepo in "Social Change and Rural Violence in Colombia," *Studies in Comparative International Development*, 4.12 (1968–69): 273: "In underdeveloped countries . . . the number of candidates for jobs in government bureaucracy exceeds the number of opportunities. The employer takes advantage of this surplus in the supply of workers; he requires that the candidate possess qualities that can make the employer's own position more secure." See also Martin H. Greenberg, *Bureaucracy and Development: A Mexican Case Study* (Lexington, Mass., 1970), particularly "Making It in the Ministry," pp. 116–21.

tion, education, welfare—there is much to be lost and little to be gained by tying one's career to any specific project or activity until such time as it has been fully legitimated and in fact undertaken by higher authorities. The ambitious municipal president who decides that electrification of the poorer *barrios* is the true test of the success of his administration is likely to find himself not only frustrated but politically disadvantaged if that goal is not fully shared by those to whom he owes his office and to whom he must apply for the resources needed to make even minimal progress.

The second way in which centralism and the characteristic leader-follower relationships of Mexican politics affect the content of public policy is to devalue expertise and planning. The pattern of rapid rotation in office and the use of thousands of positions in the government/Party apparatus as a patronage system designed to stabilize and maintain existing political arrangements are incompatible with a continuing and creative focus on problems of public policy. Not only is expert knowledge sacrificed to political expediency, but people move so fast through a series of posts that have little in common (except their political characteristics and possibilities) that few careerists develop any substantial attachment to or base of knowledge about a given domain of public policy. When this situation is compounded by the increased opportunities for corruption and avoidance of responsibility that are presented by the rotational system (one does not have to stay and answer for one's performance; deficiencies can always be blamed on past incumbents), the stage is set for the further erosion of attention to the substance of public policy. In fact, it can be argued that any rationalization or coordination of Mexican public policy that might result from centralization is lost through the corruption, inefficiency, and personalistic careerism that are the other side of the centralism coin. Thus maintaining the system has priority over planning for development, and patronage over expert performance.

Finally, there is what might be called the syndrome of *plazismo* (plaza-ism). Especially at the local level, rapid rotation in office, scarcity of resources, unwillingness to take risks, and personal ambition untempered by the necessity of standing for election combine to produce an inordinate number of public projects with low developmental importance.[12] Typically, these take the form of a "beautification" effort: an improvement to the central plaza, a new fountain, benches, paved areas, stalls, or some other civic addition of marginal usefulness. The attractions of such projects to cautious officeholders are legion: they are physically and politically visible; they can be completed in a relatively short time and thus accrue wholly to the reputational capital of the incumbent; they are for all the people and thus require no hard choices as to what sector or project should receive scarce resources; they are uncontroversial in the tradition of "good works"; they can often be partially funded through the donations of others eager to have their names associated with civic improvements. *Plazismo* results in projects that although often charming, seldom add up to a significant achievement. Above all, when energies are so engaged, both planning and serious attention to the key problems of public policy suffer. Symbols replace substance in the developmental domain.

The Government, the PRI, and the Management of Conflict

The notion of the government/Party apparatus as used to this point tends to obscure important characteristics of the relationship between the PRI and the government. Although from one point of view the government and the Party are properly seen as constituting a single instrumentality of rule, it is equally important to emphasize that the PRI serves the government in sev-

---

[12] Further up the hierarchy, a state-wide program of improvement in public markets might be undertaken by a governor eager to demonstrate to the powers in Mexico City his commitment to the masses. Although such a project might not—from the planner's point of view—have top priority, it is at least qualitatively different from building a fountain. There is a general expectation that men who command significant public resources will use some fraction of them in developmental improvements. Thus, within the tradition of *plazismo*, there is a certain pressure toward concern with public policy when the office in question is of the kind and size to suggest that the incumbent's performance should be judged by developmental as well as caretaker criteria.

eral important ways that in fact depend on the maintenance of a separate institutional identity. The PRI is not a locus of decisional power or responsibility, but it does provide critical services that enable governmental elites to maintain and exercise their decisional prerogatives. In short, as elaborated below, it functions as recruiter, broker, and integrator for the executive-centered governmental institutions.

Let us examine first the recruiting functions. Recruiting in this context means more than simply attracting talented individuals into Party posts. It also means co-opting into the officialdom of the PRI those who have already demonstrated political strength or potentiality and who therefore constitute some threat to the hegemony of the apparatus. The sequence of recruitment is thus crucial. In the domains of labor, peasant affairs, education, and economics, the Party is constantly in search of individuals who have in some fashion already distinguished themselves (*desta-cados*). Whether such persons already hold nominal membership in the Party, are "nonpolitical," or are identified with oppositional groups is of little importance. What matters is that they are potentially threatening and thus must not be allowed to build public careers outside the government/Party apparatus. The easiest way to insure that this does not happen is to invite them —no matter what their backgrounds—into lower- or middle-level Party positions (or directly into government office), thus tying them into the career-advancement game. Each such nascent político thus snared attests to the powerful pull of working within the apparatus as opposed to the difficulties of achieving any kind of public career from outside.

The brokerage activities of the PRI are manifold. Through its three functional sectors (agrarian, labor, and popular) and its multiplicity of committees and affiliates, the Party both organizes the masses for structured participation in the political process and distributes various forms of welfare benefits and patronage. In the articulation of demands and the distribution of services and sinecures, the PRI is frequently oriented toward the lower socioeconomic strata. It is precisely these groups that are most in need of jobs, welfare, and neighborhood improvements, and the Party serves as a decentralized clearinghouse through which such particularistic demands can be articulated and, at times, attended to. The socially and economically more advantaged not only do not usually need the jobs, welfare, and neighborhood improvements the Party can provide, but also as a rule do not need the Party as an intermediary between them and officialdom, for they have their own connections. Thus, the Party mediates primarily between the lower sectors of society and government, softening, personalizing, and making more responsive what might otherwise loom as an impossibly forbidding system.

It need hardly be emphasized that the Party's motives in becoming thus both mediator and benefactor are not entirely public-spirited. Just as quasi-independent leaders are a threat to the decisional hegemony of the government/Party apparatus, so unorganized and dissatisfied masses are a threat to the stability and orderly functioning of that apparatus. A strong sense of elite pragmatism coupled with an equally strong desire to control as much of the politically relevant environment as possible is evident in the arrangements just described. The operative rule is clear: if there is going to be public participation in the political process, particularly a continuous drumbeat of demands, it is much better to have that activity filtered through the political apparatus rather than resonating outside. The Party has been assigned responsibility for ensuring that this is the case. This is part of the general rule whereby the Party protects the government by assuming organizational and control duties that would otherwise require direct governmental action, and perhaps jeopardize the government's reputation. The organizing, channeling, and servicing of popular demands thus have a manipulative and exploitative side. But there is also another side. Demands, especially those that are particularistic and modest, are heard and often met, enhancing the decentralized responsive capacity of the system. To date, the distribution of bread, circuses, and other symbolic and material payoffs has been sufficient to appease or enlist at least the tacit cooperation of most important groups in Mexico.

The recruitment and brokerage functions of the PRI both sustain and derive from the Party's overriding role as the prime nongovernmental integrative mechanism of the Mexican political community. Because of the tumultuous and even fratricidal history of political conflict in Mexico, the notion that political participation must be limited is rather widely accepted both by elites and by those sectors of the masses whose opinions may be said to count. This notion was reinforced recently by the Madrazo experiment in democracy within the PRI. In many municipios the primary elections for candidates to represent the PRI proved so divisive—bringing into the public arena potentially antagonistic persons and factions that had previously coexisted under the banner of Party unity—that the experiment was abandoned.[13]

The Party operates as integrator in several ways. In any conflict, whether along class and economic lines, between labor and management, or between some other factions or interest groups, the Party is supposed to provide an arena in which the antagonists can interact to resolve their differences, if not on an equal footing at least on common ground. This is, of course, an ideal—embodied in the slogan *Todos somos Mexicanos*—that works only imperfectly in practice.[14] Nevertheless, pursuit of the ideal has vital consequences for public life in Mexico. The sectoral organization of the Party is the institutionalized expression of a long search for political structures consonant with the ideal, and Party primaries are another expression of the search—one that never became institutionalized.

Additionally, the PRI is important in coordinating the district,

[13] See Ugalde, "Conflict and Consensus," pp. 315–26 (Ensenada); and W. V. D'Antonio and Richard Suter, "Elecciones preliminares en un municipio mexicano: nuevas tendencias en la lucha de México hacia la democracia," *Revista Mexicana de Sociología*, 29.1 (Jan.–March 1967): 93–108 (Ciudad Juárez).

[14] See, for example, Graham; Grimes and Simmons; and Henry E. Torres-Trueba, "Factionalism in a Mexican Municipio," *Sociologus*, 19.2 (1969): 134–52.

municipal, state and federal levels of the apparatus. It provides the arena and the channels necessary for reconciling the activities and ambitions of a great diversity of politicians, bureaucrats, decisional centers, and special groups. For example, elections involve first a massive semiprivate sorting out of claimants to office, and then an impressive public attempt to mobilize the citizenry under the banner of the Party. The nominating process is one in which a host of conflicting claims to office, patronage, and attention must be adjudicated in a fashion that leaves the apparatus better integrated than before, whereas the campaign itself—if all goes well—should have a similar effect on the general public.[15] Elections are not, of course, the only occasions on which the Party performs this function, but at no other time are its integrative role and responsibilities so much in evidence or so fully tested.

The Dynamics of Inequality

Except for a few utopians primarily concerned with the governance of small communities, most theorists have admitted inequality into their conceptions of the political order. That is, citizens are seen as differentially endowed with participatory resources—social standing, wealth, wisdom, knowledge, experience, energy—and thus although all might be entitled to equal power or influence or benefits, such cannot in practice be the case. All real political systems also take cognizance of this fact in one way or another, some trying to reduce its consequences and others accepting it as an empirical necessity or even celebrating it as an ethical imperative. In Mexico, where constitutional commitment to the reduction of inequality is quite strong, there has emerged a classic tension between this prescriptive

[15] In addition to the literature cited previously, see Barry Ames, "Bases of Support for Mexico's Dominant Party," *American Political Science Review*, 44.1 (March 1970): 153–67; Robert K. Furtak, "El Partido Revolucionario Institucional: Integración nacional y movilización electoral," *Foro Internacional*, 9.4, (April–June 1969): 339–53; Karl Schmitt, "Congressional Campaigning in Mexico: A View from the Provinces," *Journal of Inter-American Studies*, 11.1 (Jan. 1969): 93–110.

ideal and the empirical reality of a system that is sharply stratified with respect not only to who governs, but also to who benefits. Although the tension is as much intellectual as political—
at least the discrepancies between rhetoric and reality do not
agitate public life so as to command widespread and consistent
attention—one cannot easily dismiss the issue. Not only is the
gap between the prescribed order and the actual order dramatically wide, but the latter generates certain dynamics that make
increased equality of participation and benefits less rather than
more likely.

The centralized decisional system of Mexico and the sharply
stratified pattern of participatory resources that go with it are
only part of the panorama of inequality. Also central to our concerns is the dynamic of inequality that can be seen in governmental responsiveness and the distribution of benefits. Although
the two processes are clearly related—in that the style of decision-making is one of the prime determinants of the pattern of
distribution—the latter can profitably be considered separately.

One of the most frequently recurring themes in the literature
on Mexico is that the substantial aggregate growth of the economy over the past three decades has benefited regions and
classes very unequally. The regulated although essentially market economy of Mexico operates to give advantages and rewards
to the city as opposed to the countryside, the northern states
and the Federal District (Mexico City and environs) as opposed
to the central and southern states, and the upper and middle
classes as opposed to the workers and peasants.[16] The counter-

[16] To some extent workers and peasants have actually subsidized growth
through declines not only in their share of total income, but in their real
wages. Estimates of the percentage of the Mexican population that has been
so hurt vary from about 20 percent to about 50 percent. See Alonso Aguilar
M. and Fernando Carmona, *México: riqueza y miseria* (Mexico: Editorial
Nuestro Tiempo, 1967); Oscar Lewis, "Mexico Since Cardenas," in Richard
N. Adams *et al.*, *Social Change in Latin America Today* (New York, 1960);
Ifigenia M. de Navarrete, "Income Distribution in Mexico," in Enrique
Pérez López *et al.*, *Mexico's Recent Economic Growth* (University of Texas
Press, 1967); Morris Singer, *Growth, Equality, and the Mexican Experience*
(University of Texas Press, 1969); and the essays on Mexico in Joseph A.
Kahl, ed., *Comparative Perspectives on Stratification: Mexico, Great Britain,*

point of riches and misery that draws the attention of almost every student of modern Mexico is the outcome of processes that have gone on for decades. Overall economic growth in Mexico has not brought about a more equitable distribution of goods and services. Quite the contrary, it has been functionally related to the maintenance and in some instances the intensification of existing inequalities.

Rhetoric and good intentions aside, the net redistributive impact of government activity over the past few decades has probably not been great. The "natural" flow of goods, services, and benefits to those most able to pay for them is at least partially reinforced by the capacity of these same sectors to perpetuate their conditions of life through quasi-political means. Whether it is states that because of their economic strength and political importance are able to secure a disproportionate amount of public investment,[17] or groups such as the elite unions that because of their scarce skills and their corporate political representation are able to gain more than an equal share of wage increases and other benefits, or residents of the wealthier and more influential *colonias* (neighborhoods) who command urban services that are elsewhere in short supply, the political process tends to reinforce the distributional patterns of the market.

In this, Mexico does not differ from most other systems. Advantages accumulate; because of location and the control of relevant resources, certain regions, groups, and individuals can ensure that they continue to get more than their share of benefits. But the corrective forces, the counter-dynamics that operate in

---

Japan (Boston, 1968). As Clark W. Reynolds points out in *The Mexican Economy: Twentieth-Century Structure and Growth* (Yale University Press, 1970), p. 75, income inequality in Mexico is acute even by the general standards of less developed countries. In India, for example, it was estimated that the lowest three quintiles (60 percent) of the population were receiving about 28 percent of all personal income in the 1950's. In Mexico the corresponding figure was 21.5 percent in 1963, down from 24.6 percent in 1950!

[17] See Wilkie, Part 2; and Paul W. Drake, "Mexican Regionalism Reconsidered," *Journal of Inter-American Studies and World Affairs*, 12.3 (July 1970): 401–15.

some systems, are weak or nonexistent in Mexico. That is, the political process does not give the underprivileged sufficient power to redress imbalances. Much as it may now be fashionable to scoff at competitive party politics and elections, historically they have worked to the relative advantage of those who have little else except their votes with which to do battle against privilege. In England, the United States, and other countries, certain kinds of social and economic inequalities were reduced by the extension of the franchise in the context of meaningful and competitive elections. In Mexico, however, the institutionalization of party life and elections serves not to increase the power of the underclasses, but rather to ensure that their votes and their energies help to maintain existing distributive patterns. And with extra-constitutional means of protest closed or extremely costly to them, the redress of imbalances thus takes place at the pleasure of the elites—slowly, if at all.[18]

The mutually reinforcing aspects of economic and political inequality can be seen at work in almost any municipio in Mexico. Because of the fiscal weakness of municipal government, it is quite common for the citizens of a barrio or a colonia to be asked to help finance basic urban services such as street improvements and electrification. Clearly, the more substantial colonias are better able to tax themselves—or be taxed—and thus more likely to secure matching funds and resources from the state or local government. When these funds and resources are as scarce as they usually are in Mexico, every project undertaken in an already advantaged area must in a real sense be counted as withheld from a disadvantaged area. Furthermore, even when no local contributions are needed, the more prosperous colonias are the more likely to contain residents with political and bureaucratic connections and skills and thus the more likely to receive any scarce urban services that are distributed as patronage. Finally, since withholding or switching the vote is not a meaningful threat, little pressure can be brought to bear

[18] See Evelyn P. Stevens, "Legality and Extra-Legality in Mexico," *Journal of Inter-American Studies and World Affairs*, 12.1 (Jan. 1970): 62–75.

To each his own, and to the movies for most. For the reader who is unfamiliar with Mexican politics, and particularly with Mexican political stereotypes, the four parties depicted here might be characterized as follows: PRI (Partido Revolucionario Institucional), filler of the patronage trough; PAN (Partido de Acción Nacional), the "haves"; PPS (Partido Popular Socialista), the "approved" Left; PARM (Partido Auténtico de la Revolución Mexicana), the geriatric Right, approved by the PRI.

by the underclasses except as they convince party officials of the rightness of their demands or at least of the prudence of granting them in the interest of maintaining public order.

Citizens and Support

Public support of the Mexican government is substantial. The few national interview studies that have been conducted show that the overwhelming majority of politically conscious Mexicans are positively allegiant to the nation, whatever criticisms and complaints they may have about specific institutions, practices, and men.[19] However, it has also been argued—sometimes on the basis of the same data—that what the masses "give" to the system is not their support in any positive sense but rather their acquiescence, often expressed in noninvolvement and apathy. These two perspectives are not at all incompatible; both provide important, albeit partial, views of popular orientations to politics. Both are part of the prevalent syndrome of allegiance to *lo mexicano*, ritual participation, passivity, and withdrawal. Although this syndrome may not fit the usual conceptions of what the good citizen ought to believe and do, it fits very well into ongoing patterns of governance in Mexico.

Thus, *support* will be construed rather loosely here. In particular, it is assumed that what some might consider ritualistic engagement in a wide range of institutions and practices (or refusal to challenge those institutions and practices) is critical to the maintenance of the government/Party apparatus and may therefore be considered support. The norms, values, and attitudes that sustain such patterns of engagement and acquiescence constitute a massive if diffuse grant of legitimacy to the Mexican regime by its citizens. Moreover, the grant is made with

[19] See Gabriel A. Almond and Sidney Verba, *The Civic Culture: Political Attitudes and Democracy in Five Nations* (Princeton University Press, 1963); and Joseph A. Kahl, *The Measurement of Modernism* (University of Texas Press, 1968). It should be noted that this majority is partially offset by a small but politically active minority whose hostility in its most intense form is expressed in guerrilla and terroristic opposition to the regime, activities that increased in Mexico during the late 1960's.

little expectation and few promises of anything in return, giving elites considerable room to maneuver even when dealing with more or less organized groups. Mexico is a system in which there is a great deal of this sort of flexibility.

What is thus more generally at issue is the part played by various sectors of the public in the governance of Mexico. When a group or organization seeks specific benefits or advantages from political decision-makers, the relationship of that group to the political process is relatively clear. What we are arguing is that this interest-group model explains only a limited range of citizen attitudes and behaviors in Mexico, and perhaps an even more limited range of elite behavior and system attributes. Stated differently, we emphasize the importance of non-demanding groups, sectors that typically do not try to influence the decisional process or compete for leadership roles but rather behave and participate in ways that enable politics-as-usual to continue. This "enabling participation" is founded on a complex of norms, values, and attitudes widely shared among Mexican citizens. Understanding this complex, its relationship to such participation, and its role in the conduct of Mexican politics is a central purpose of our analysis.

Without going into detail on the manner in which Mexican citizens relate to the political process, it is nevertheless useful here to hypothesize, on the basis of the work of others, two key aspects of the content and patterning of beliefs and behavior. First, as already suggested, Mexicans often subscribe to quite incongruent normative and descriptive models of the system of which they are a part. Although allegiant to the larger system, proud of its accomplishments, and optimistic about the future, citizens frequently describe and evaluate the daily operation of that system in the most negative terms. This incongruence is easily seen, whether in the peasant who calls the PRI the Party of the *Robolución (robo* means "robbery"), or in Kahl's mill foreman who "believes that Mexico is moving forward, and . . . approves of general government policies . . . yet in every personal experience with politicians . . . has found them crooked or useless, [and] thus . . . believes in a government whose representatives he distrusts."[20] This incongruence, however, does not necessarily imply either psychological pressure toward its own resolution or increasing levels of opposition to the government. In other words, for reasons that will be explored subsequently, most Mexicans live easily with their seemingly contradictory views of politics, continuing to behave in ways that enable the government/Party apparatus to maintain its centralized style of rule.

There is also widespread public acceptance of existing inequalities and stratification patterns. In a line of corporatist thinking that goes back to Plato and St. Thomas it has been argued that recognition and acceptance of one's station is the key to the good society when individual endowments vary and resources and opportunities are limited. The principles of society and government brought to the New World by the Spaniards were very much in this tradition, emphasizing hierarchy and inequality in both the socioeconomic and the political order and encouraging people to accept the personal situations that resulted. Moreover, this tradition has shown impressive staying power, manifesting itself not only in the colonial but in the Independence and national periods, and in settings otherwise as diverse as Mexico and Chile.[21]

Although contemporary Mexican political rhetoric is closer to the libertarian tradition than to this corporatist world view, there is still much in both the theory and the practice of Mexican politics that more nearly fits the latter. Not only are the structure and stability of the Mexican system involved, but moral issues are obviously raised when a system of sharp inequalities

[20] Kahl, *The Measurement of Modernism*, p. 116. Local characterizations of the PRI as "El Partido de la Robolución" are discussed in Torres-Trueba. See also Almond and Verba, pp. 414–28, and Scott, "Mexico: The Established Revolution."

[21] See Richard M. Morse, "The Heritage of Latin America," in Louis Hartz, ed., *The Founding of New Societies* (New York, 1964). Morse's rich and suggestive essay rightly emphasizes that the Mexican Revolution and the system that evolved in its aftermath are deeply consonant with the Hispanic tradition, despite the seeming originality of certain ideas and arrangements.

is legitimated by the beliefs of those who are most deprived. Thus in the pages that follow we shall pay substantial attention to social, economic, and political stratification, their correlates, consequences, and acceptance by different groups and sectors of the population. It is one of the partial paradoxes involved in studying modern Mexico that although classical models relating social class to politics are not particularly illuminating, an understanding of socioeconomic stratification is nevertheless central to an appreciation of how the political system works.[22] In other words, precisely because inequalities are so glaring and class-based political movements are so weak, much remains to be explained. In the chapter that follows we shall begin our explanation with an analysis of political institutions and processes in Jalapa, turning in subsequent chapters to an exploration of the behavior, beliefs, and orientations that sustain them.

[22] This point is well made by Pablo González Casanova, "Dynamics of Class Structure," in Kahl, *Comparative Perspectives on Stratification,* especially pp. 73–82.

Three

Governing Jalapa

The general characteristics of Mexican politics sketched in the previous chapter are all apparent and operative in Jalapa. One of them is, in fact, the most striking characteristic of local politics: the extent to which participation by citizens in political recruitment and in all stages of policy-making is controlled. Thus, although Jalapeños are not excluded from the political arena, they are typically admitted only when conditions suit the purposes of those who manage the public domain. The system does not always work perfectly, as materials in this chapter attest, but it works well enough to create a smoothly operating political process.

A second striking characteristic of Jalapan politics is that there is often an uncoupling of access and influence. Those who are active and get opportunities to make their preferences known, whether through institutional channels such as the PRI or in more personalistic ways, do not always have more influence than those "who only stand and wait." Actually, both types of citizens can be seen as reinforcing the power of the established government/Party apparatus, the one by participating and thus legitimizing or contributing resources to existing decisions, and the other by withdrawing from the public arena and thus not challenging these decisions. The system of administering the political process that results is thus both self-perpetuating and relatively well insulated from public pressure. It falters only when

programs cannot be put into effect without the active cooperation of the citizens, and it breaks down temporarily only when
the opposition cannot be bought or frightened off. Usually, however, controlled participation, a mixture of symbolic and material payoffs, withdrawal from politics by most citizens, and consequently wide latitude for the elites in making decisions are
the norms.

But before getting into the details of this system of controlled
access, marginal participation, and limited response, it is necessary to have a more complete understanding of local political
institutions. Once this is accomplished, we will then turn our attention to the citizens of Jalapa, their claims on government,
their various ways of expressing these claims, the manner in
which public officials respond to them, and the latent agenda of
local problems that citizens perceive as most critical.

The Structure of Government

Local government in Jalapa shares basic structural features with
the state and federal governments, and the PRI is divided into
sectors in the municipio, just as it is in the state of Veracruz and
in the nation. The pattern of allotment of government posts to
sector representatives is found at all levels, and recruitment, including the process whereby nominations for safe elective posts
are distributed, is everywhere the same.

An understanding of the politics of Jalapa must begin with the
state government, for its leaders and their agents repeatedly appear as key factors in the operation of nominally local organizations. The governor serves for a six-year term and, like all other
elected officials, cannot succeed himself. Although subsequently
voted into office, he is in fact chosen by the President of Mexico,
with little regard for public opinion. He combines elements of a
political boss with those of an administrator whose extensive
community influence is almost certain to disappear at the end of
his term in office.

The governor not only chooses his administrative aides (his
private secretary, heads and subchiefs of government ministries,

etc.), but also dominates the selection of the 14 deputies of the single-branch state legislature. The latter are all PRI members who, given the governor's nod, are dutifully nominated by their respective regional PRI organizations and then ratified in the general election.[1] They rarely forget their obligation to the incumbent governor, and carefully follow his leadership. The largely symbolic state and federal legislative posts are always divided among the popular, labor, and agrarian sectors of the PRI. These allocations are most relevant for the latter two, because they are so poorly represented in executive positions. The resulting centralism was nicely summarized by an ex-mayor of Jalapa in reply to a question about political influence: "Look! people are not influential as individuals. All together they form a group, supported by the 'sun.' The 'sun' is the governor. He imposes, defines the lines of battle, shapes the ideas. Yes, the governor is the voice they listen to, and the others are satellites revolving to the rhythm he marks."[2]

The statewide PRI organization is formally capped by its State Directive Committee. The Committee's president is the only member selected with significant out-of-state intervention, in this case by the national PRI. The secretary-general and the treasurer of the Committee are the only full-time employee-officers; they are selected by and owe allegiance to the governor. In 1966, among the eight "secretaries" for specific realms of Party activity such as agrarian affairs, workers' affairs, women's affairs, there were two state deputies, two middle-ranking state officials,

[1] Most of these officeholders are relatively young, college-educated males (the average age except for the governor himself and the few chiefs of ministries is probably less than 40). Many have studied law; most, although not born in Jalapa, have lived there for years either because they attended the university or because they worked in the city.

[2] In addition to the above-mentioned survey of 399 adults, we conducted interviews with a number of Jalapans who, often by virtue of past or present high official position, could be considered quite knowledgeable about the city. An English translation of the basic questionnaire used in these elite informant interviews is included in Appendix B. Other information about these interviews (including a list of the occupations and positions of the 55 primary informants) is included in Appendix C.

a representative from the major organization within the agrarian sector, the League of Agrarian Communities affiliated within the *Confederación Nacional Campesina* (CNC), another from the popular sector organized under the *Confederación Nacional de Organizaciones Populares* (CNOP), and representatives from two of the three major labor federations, the *Confederación de Trabajadores Mexicanos* (CTM), and the *Confederación Regional de Obreros Mexicanos* (CROM).[3] Similar patterns of representation appear one step lower in the hierarchy, in Jalapa's ayuntamiento and in the Municipal Committee of the PRI.

Ayuntamiento commonly has two meanings, though in context little confusion results. It refers to the collective body of elected municipal officials, the mayor and six other council members; it is also used to designate the institution of municipal government (the council and its various administrative departments). The mayor (*presidente municipal*), the first and second vice-presidents (*síndicos*), and four regular councilmen (*regidores*) all serve concurrent three-year terms. One other prominent official is the secretary, a man appointed by the mayor and the one who normally bears much of the latter's routine administrative burdens. All these incumbents receive full salaries, which, with the possible exception of the mayor's, normally represent more compensation for less work than those they received in their regular occupations. The mayor's post usually goes to a career politician, and only he among council members has any political stature. The other six councilmen are drawn from various local organizations, following the norm of sectoral representation.

The municipal recruitment process is most lively at three-year intervals when, beginning months before the PRI nomination will be settled, aspirants to the mayor's post try to build support and impress the governor. In the words of one such aspirant and former secretary to the ayuntamiento, they "look for useful contacts and sound out their friends and acquaintances." Late in

[3] No single organization represents the labor sector as the CNC and CNOP represent the agrarian and popular sectors.

"Elections? How thrilling!"

the summer the governor's choice becomes known informally. That individual, the *destapado* (roughly meaning the "unveiled one"), is then publicly endorsed by local PRI affiliates and soon thereafter is formally nominated by the Party's municipal committee. A few weeks of "campaigning" follow, during which the official candidate is exposed to the public in his new role. In September the formality of a general election is observed, and the new mayor is elected without competition and with relatively few votes cast.[4]

Though he will dominate politics within the ayuntamiento, in the broader context the mayor's powers are very limited. The ayuntamiento institution is weak, and the man picked to head it is normally neither a strong leader nor a popular one. In fact, it is widely believed among local and state politicians that no governor would tolerate an active, popular, or flamboyant mayor in Jalapa, because such a leader would inevitably detract from the governor's prestige and power in his own capital. This belief would seem to be well supported by the facts. In short, in Jalapa today there is no place for a local *cacique*. The mayor acts on the basis of the authority given him by the government/PRI regime, and his personal influence and political style are thus circumscribed. This situation was well captured in a comment by an important businessman-lawyer from the city: "It's no longer pos-

---

[4] The weakness of the PAN (Partido de Acción Nacional) in Jalapa leaves PRI candidates without any opposition. This is not the usual case in the larger cities of Mexico.

sible for us to have a tough-guy mayor, wearing a Texas-style hat, with a pistol stuck in his belt, and pushing everybody around. That type is becoming rarer all the time, above all in important cities like the state capitals." Not long ago, a mayor of Jalapa did draw a gun on one of his more vociferous political critics (despite efforts to eliminate the practice, men still sometimes carry guns hidden beneath their clothing). No shots were fired, however, and the hot-headed mayor was strongly reprimanded by the governor.

Because Jalapa is regarded as a predominantly white-collar or bureaucratic community, the mayor is always identified with the middle class and selected from the Party's popular sector. Allocation of the remaining ayuntamiento posts follows a relatively consistent pattern whereby labor representatives fill three or four places, the agrarian sector one, and the popular sector one or two. Recruitment to these six lesser offices is more open than for the mayoralty, primarily because the governor is less concerned with them and allows greater latitude to the selection process within the PRI. The selection rewards individuals and organizations for party loyalty and, in some cases, for service to prominent politicians. The following synopsis of local recruitment practices was offered by one informant, a federal bureaucrat of long residence in Jalapa: "Here in Jalapa there has been the unfortunate custom that the president of the ayuntamiento is picked by the governor, and the rest [of its offices] are distributed by the Party. This process can be regarded as distribution of the booty of war: X group receives a regidor, Y group another regidor, Z group a síndico, etc. They claim to be sending representatives and, as a rule, do not send their best men."

Some notion of the limited functions of municipal government in Mexico was presented in the preceding chapter as part of the description of centralism. Jalapa is hardly an exception, for few if any major decisions originate in the ayuntamiento. For the most part, it merely carries out the policies of the state government, collects taxes, administers the city-owned markets, and maintains and improves ongoing community services. The only

TABLE 3.1

Projected Ayuntamiento Expenditures, 1955–66

Category of expenditure	1955	1963	1964	1965	1966
Wages, salaries, and benefits:					
Officials and employees	38%	33%	42%	37%	48%
School personnel[a]	16	14	14	12	12
General operating expenses	31	35	27	29	18
Obrería Mayor: discretionary funds,					
going mostly to public works	4	9	9	16	14
Subsidies to welfare agencies	4	5	5	4	5
Subsidies to political, labor, sports, and					
cultural organizations	2	1	1	2	3[b]
Miscellaneous and other	5	3	2	0	0
TOTAL	100%	100%	100%	100%	100%
Total projected budget:					
Pesos (millions)	1.34	4.50	5.00	7.00	8.50[c]
Dollars (thousands)	107	360	400	560	680

SOURCE: Calculated from reports on file with the state legislature.

[a] Most public schools are supported and run by the state government; the ayuntamiento supports only a few elementary schools.

[b] The 1966 budget included subsidies of 1,200 pesos (96 dollars) each to the state and local CROC and the national, state, and local CTM, the Union of Municipal Employees, the League of Agrarian Communities, and other organizations.

[c] This is approximately 90 pesos or $7.20 U.S. per capita.

significant break in routine occurs when a public works project such as the reconstruction of a street is planned and undertaken.

Recent municipal budgets, like those presented in Table 3.1, reflect this concentration on maintenance, regulation, and caretaking.[5] Most years, salaries and benefits to officials and employees exceed one-third of the total. When local teachers paid by the municipio are added to this total, more than one-half of the budget is usually accounted for. The ambiguous category of "general operating expenses" takes anywhere from a fifth to a third of all allocations, and the only remaining item of consequence is the discretionary fund (which is largely used for public works). Furthermore, despite a dramatic increase over the decade in the absolute size of the budget, priorities have

[5] Many official budgetary data are irretrievable soon after the reports are filed. For municipal budgets the best data were in state archives. These consisted of projected ayuntamiento budgets as approved by the state legislature. Actual expenditures were found for only two years.

TABLE 3.2

Projected Ayuntamiento Revenue, Fiscal 1963
(*Percent*)

Source of revenue	Projection
Taxes, all based on a percentage of the corresponding state tax (largest single source, 25%, was tax on commerce and industry, followed by tax on urban residential property)	59%
Fees and licenses (public markets, cemetery, slaughterhouse, etc.)	24
Other fees (street vendors, street cleaning, fines, etc.)	13
Rebates from certain state and federal taxes (e.g., on alcohol sold locally)	2
Rent from buildings and equipment, and miscellaneous	2
TOTAL	100%

SOURCE: Calculated from reports on file with the state legislature. The total projected revenue was 4.5 million pesos.

changed hardly at all.[6] Budgetary increases do not stem from and are not reflected in new community services; they reflect better pay and increased benefits for those who are giving the community "more of the same."

Furthermore, as the distribution of projected sources of revenue for 1963 suggests (Table 3.2) the ayuntamiento is very much constrained in raising money. The taxes it levies are limited by law to a certain percentage of existing state taxes; it gets almost no rebates from the monies the state collects in the municipio; it floats no bonds; and—as we shall see later in this chapter—there are sharp political limitations on the extent to which citizens can be assessed for local improvements and programs.

Not surprisingly, in the light of local fiscal and decisional limitations, most important public services in Jalapa originate with organizations other than those controlled by municipal government. Electricity is supplied by the Comisión Federal de Elec-

[6] Increases in revenue have come primarily from general growth and from more effective enforcement of existing taxes rather than from new legislation or new sources of income. Nevertheless, significant tax-enforcement problems remain. As one informant, a businessman, put it, "It is almost a question of honor for a Mexican to avoid payment of taxes."

tricidad (CFE), a federal monopoly. Until mid-1966 the water system was exclusively controlled by another federal agency, the Secretaría de Recursos Hidraúlicos, and federal dominance subsequently continued despite a reorganization that led to a tripartite administrative board with one representative each from municipal, state, and federal governments. The community abounds with police facilities, primarily because of the presence of the state government. The ayuntamiento supervises a quasi-police night-watchman force paid for by residents, and also employs a very small police contingent contracted for from the state. A separately organized and state-run police force is responsible for traffic. The state and federal governments operate most of the schools, and the content of all public instruction below the university level is carefully controlled by the federal government. Finally, there is a local Junta de Mejoramiento Moral, Cívico, y Material (Board for Moral, Civic, and Material Improvement). Ostensibly, it is a politically autonomous committee of private citizens who work with both the public and government to promote community improvements; actually, it is now closely tied to state government.

The state of Veracruz and especially its capital city are PRI strongholds, and although sympathizers for other parties certainly can be found in Jalapa, only the PRI is fully organized and operative throughout the year. Neither of the two minor parties, the conservative PAN and the leftist Partido Popular Socialista (PPS), mounts any effective opposition. Locally, the PRI is headed by a municipal committee, wherein sectoral representation again is the norm, but not unexpectedly this committee finds itself overshadowed by and largely at the service of the State Directive Committee. In fact, in 1966, just before a new PRI state office building was opened, the municipal committee's "office" consisted of a desk in the office of the state committee. Most of the municipal organization's activities occur at election time and during the Party's occasional membership drives.

Membership in the PRI is elastic both in terms of numbers and conceptualization. Citing a mimeographed document designated as an official record of registered voters, the state secretary-general of the PRI claimed approximately 30,000 Party members for Jalapa in 1966, 17,000 men and 13,000 women. Perhaps the fact that the PRI at that moment was engaged in a nation-wide membership drive occasioned that astronomically high claim, equal to roughly two-thirds of the adult population.[7] Responses to our survey suggest that 11 percent membership among adults would be the most accurate estimate. Two other factors also help to explain the extraordinary claim. First, membership figures were undoubtedly greatly inflated by the inclusion of all government employees and union members. Relatively few of those people ever deliberately affiliated themselves, although some at least realize that they are counted as members. Others, however, do not even think of themselves as Party members, and only a minority pays dues or is active in any significant fashion. Second, the official claim probably includes many young people loosely associated with the youth section of the PRI but too young to be included in our survey and not yet of voting age.

Access, Communication, and Groups

Whether it is one man's quest for a job, a neighborhood group's petition for better drainage facilities, opposition by the Chamber of Commerce to itinerant vendors, or any other of the multitudinous claims brought before government, certain general procedures and styles characterize the communication of political interests in Jalapa. Most important, the flow of such communications tends to concentrate at higher levels because of decisional centralism. In Jalapa, to be more specific, all important decisions about public affairs (except matters of clear federal jurisdic-

---

[7] Affiliation drives probably result in large increases in nominal membership. For example, in Ensenada, the CRT labor federation (*Confederación Revolucionaria de Trabajadores*) received the following instructions from its national headquarters: "The Executive Committees of each union and of each member organization of the CRT will be responsible for affiliating to the PRI all the members of its group. . . . We recommend that this work of affiliation be completed as soon as possible, and it should include not only the workers of our unions and associations, but also all relatives who are of age." Antonio Ugalde, "Conflict and Consensus," pp. 81–82.

tion), and a great many not-so-crucial decisions are made by the state government. Most citizens are well aware that the state authorities usually decide, and only the least resourceful waste much energy on the mayor and his aides. Moreover, the proximity of state leaders detracts from the political brokerage function that the mayor might otherwise perform. To be on the safe side, of course, community groups often do communicate their relevant interests to the ayuntamiento, but at the same time they commonly contact those who are higher up in quest of additional support or favorable intervention. Many times, however, well connected groups and individuals simply skip municipal authorities in pursuit of direct state-level support. A similar pattern exists in relation to the PRI organization. The PRI Municipal Committee is frequently bypassed in favor of direct communication with the ayuntamiento or, better still, with either the PRI State Directive Committee or high state government officials themselves (who often, of course, are on the State Committee).

The style of communication must be cautious. Interested parties are aware of considerable sensitivity about status among public officials, and usually phrase their requests accordingly. The communication of deference is an important element of such transactions, especially as the socioeconomic or political distance between the petitioner and his official contact grows. State politics draws a large number of politicians and would-be politicians to Jalapa in nominally bureaucratic posts, and they, joined by their local counterparts, create a highly politicized *ambiente*. Preoccupied with their own political careers, they tend to relate specific events and encounters to their job prospects and fortunes. They are thus hypersensitive to demands or even discussions that might be taken to imply criticism of their performance. As two politically prominent Jalapans pointed out in discussing the way in which one ought to approach public officials:

It is possible to exchange impressions with political leaders, but unless you personally have a secure economic position it is risky to criticize government actions in front of some officials. This is true because to point out errors often is regarded as an attack on the politi-

cal regime or on the administrative system within which they operate. . . . There is a tendency, still present but diminishing with the
increasing competence of government leaders, to regard all criticism
as destructive.

Criticism of the political establishment is greatly tempered, not because of fear of physical violence, but more in order to defend one's
other interests.

Much this same spirit carries over into government relations
with the local press. In 1966 five daily papers were published in
the city. Of the five, only *El Diario de Xalapa* has a large staff
and relatively extensive news-gathering and printing facilities;
its publisher is an ex-mayor of Jalapa who has ambitions for even
higher political office. Two other papers might be called medium-sized in this context—*El Comentario* and *El Tiempo*—
while the remaining two are very small. The political content of
these papers is found in editorial commentary, news of government actions and political events, and gossip about impending
government decisions and office changes. Only *El Diario* and *El
Comentario* make a serious effort to report national and international as well as local news. Small weekly papers come and
go, often at the behest of groups within the PRI. State and local
politics are reported in the local press but not normally on radio
and television. Neither the four local radio stations nor the four
television stations received locally (three from Mexico City and
one from the city of Veracruz) carry significant news or comment on political affairs in Jalapa.

None of our community informants except the publishers
themselves assigned major significance to the press as a key
source of political information or criticism, or as a community
watchdog, for any paper that wants to survive must operate
within severe political constraints. The most immediate judge of
acceptable content is the governor, although federal authorities
are sometimes interested. An immediate consequence of this informal censorship is that no serious criticisms of the governor, of
the President, or of their major policies appear in the press. Municipal authorities are less immune to critical scrutiny, but even

the ayuntamiento can provide rewards and threats sufficient to neutralize most if not all the papers. Interestingly, these same papers express varying opinions on international issues not directly involving Mexico, and sometimes even adopt a critical stance on the details of national questions when the state and federal governments and their highest officials feel secure from scandal. The press is treading on dangerous ground, however, when it reflects badly on the performance of the existing regime, the "rules of the game," or the constitutional framework.

Techniques of censorship and press control illustrate a style of management common throughout Mexico. Of primary importance are various kinds of government subsidies, essential for the survival of most papers. Loans for capital investments (channeled through financing agencies, such as Nacional Financiera), subsidized newsprint (supplied by PIPSA, the federal newsprint monopoly), and outright payments for favorable publicity are standard procedures. Loans, usually long overdue in any case, can always be recalled, and a newsprint allotment can always be canceled or decreased. The condition for the subsidies is, of course, politically acceptable behavior. The third practice, outright payments, fills the press in Jalapa with so-called news items that are in fact little more than paid publicity. Conversely, unfavorable news items can be suppressed by such payments. A fourth type of subsidy, one very important in this and other capital cities, comes through contracts for printing jobs for government and PRI-affiliated groups.

In addition to such direct incentives and sanctions, two other mechanisms are important in the control of the local press. Publishers may have personal political ambitions, which naturally can be pursued only within the framework of the government/ PRI apparatus and its system of recruitment. Not surprisingly, therefore, such men carefully avoid editorial policies that would alienate important political leaders, especially the governor. Second, despite constitutional guarantees and political orientations that make open coercion costly in terms of community respect, the press cannot ignore the possibility of violence. Personal threats are infrequent, but destruction of equipment and disruption of distribution arrangements are not unknown. The tribulations of *El Comentario*, probably the least diplomatic and most ideologically alienated of Jalapa's papers, provide a clear example of methods of control. At one point during the term of Governor Quirasco (1956–1962) the newspaper's main printing equipment was "dismantled," allegedly because the company that had supplied the equipment had not been paid. In reality, the action was widely understood to be a reprisal instigated by the governor, who was annoyed by *El Comentario*'s editorial policy. Despite efforts to stop the action and later to retrieve the equipment or win an appropriate compensation, judicial authorities at the state level did nothing. Eventually a federal court ruled in favor of the publisher, but by 1966 no compensation had been or was likely to be given. The lesson in this case was too obvious to be lost on other publishers in Jalapa. The continued existence of *El Comentario*, however, reveals the flexibility both of the publisher and of the prevailing system. Generally, offenses to his predecessor are of no great concern to a new governor, and thus the response of Governor López Arias to *El Comentario*'s battles with Quirasco was to ignore the entire affair.

In this environment of particularistic demands, communications directed to the highest possible levels, and general sensitivity to criticism, who has more or less clearly regularized access to decision-makers? What groups get listened to and why? These are by no means easy questions to answer. With the informant data at hand we can do no more than outline the manner in which the most important groups—the business community, labor, and university students—usually relate to government.

The special interdependency between government and private enterprise in Mexico, developed over the past few decades, conditions the way businessmen are treated when they approach officials. In recent years government leaders have been especially attentive to the goals of political stability and economic growth, goals widely endorsed in the business community. Thus, despite many other differences, basic agreement on the primacy of stability and growth provides a basis for a dialogue between government and business.

Nevertheless, many Jalapan businessmen resent the formal ties that the regime maintains with labor, and they quite commonly feel at best a thinly veiled scorn for *políticos*. This is often expressed in seemingly neutral fashion as a distinction between the "political" and "private" spheres. For example, one informant said, "Private citizens and politician-types have their own separate social and intellectual lives. The two realms coexist, but without great mutual esteem and with little collaboration between them." (Off the record, he would probably have been less polite.) This gap is felt most acutely at the municipal level where *ayuntamiento* authorities can do less of tangible benefit for business and depend more on organized labor than does the state government.

As a group, however, businessmen are usually listened to by public officials if only because the commercial sector provides important government revenues and badly needed jobs. Government attentiveness in this context is roughly proportional to the particular claimant's standing in the local economy. For instance, in Jalapa the principal coffee processors (who have widespread holdings in other businesses), the few industrialists, and the largest businessmen receive more consideration than do the small and medium-sized merchants. On the other hand, the vital interests and demands of these wealthier businessmen impinge less directly on community resources and issues than would be the case for those involved in more modest enterprises. Thus the former appear as claimants less frequently. For most merchants, however, government regulation of business hours, some commodity prices, licenses, and problems involving municipal and state taxes are immediate and critical concerns. No matter how they feel about politicians, they cannot avoid mixing in the political and administrative life of the city. It is merchants of this type who are disproportionately active in organizations such as the Chamber of Commerce and in the PRI.[8] In these settings, some of the thorniest problems in allocating resources and adjudicating conflicting claims are generated, for men so affiliated are not easily ignored or directed elsewhere. This is not to say that they always or even usually get their way, but unlike the coffee families and those who own the largest enterprises, the smaller businessmen cannot depend primarily on their individual resources to get a hearing. They need and look for all the organizational help they can get, thus coming into frequent if not always harmonious contact with local officials.

What about organized labor? Almost all white-collar state and federal employees in Jalapa belong to organizations affiliated with the PRI's popular sector (CNOP) through the civil servants' union known as the FSTSE (Federación de Sindicatos de Trabajadores en el Servicio del Estado). Other governmental employees and many workers in the private sector are also members of unions. These unions are in turn affiliated with one of two state labor federations and the corresponding national confederation; all are associated with the labor sector of the PRI. The two labor federations, the CTM and the CROC (Confederación Revolucionaria de Obreros y Campesinos), also have regional branches roughly coincident with the municipio. In 1966, the CTM claimed three to four thousand members in 50 affiliated unions, while the CROC claimed approximately five thousand members in 25 affiliates in its Jalapa region.[9]

Through the resultant linked bureaucracies flow innumerable claims that might not otherwise reach government authorities at all. The importance of this means of access is not lost on the working class, which has thus gotten its foot in the door. Unfortunately, the rate of success in getting the authorities to act fa-

---

[8] By federal law all merchants with a capital investment of over 1,500 pesos ($120 U.S.) must register with the Chamber of Commerce (Cámara Nacional de Comercio). Active membership is another matter, however, and of the approximately 1,000 businessmen registered, only about 400 participate even minimally. Information supplied by the office of the Cámara Nacional de Comercio de Jalapa, Veracruz.

[9] These figures, suppled by the state offices of the respective federations, should be taken with caution.

"Unite them? I thought they were going to hang them!" Mexican readers would recognize the labor leaders in the noose, for Rius has drawn likenesses of them as they often appear in political cartoons. For instance, immediately below the knot of the noose, wearing dark glasses, is Fidel Velásquez, long-time head of the Confederación de Trabajadores Mexicanos and collaborator with Mexican governments.

vorably on such claims is usually inversely proportional to the cost of the services sought. Workers and their organizations are poor, but so in many ways is government. Responses and responsiveness are thus limited. Organized labor's political position in Jalapa is further weakened by three additional factors: widespread dependence on government employment; competition between the CTM and the CROC, whose rivalry increases the governor's strength in dealing with each; and the dominance of labor leaders who are themselves severely compromised by their personal stake in state politics. Thus labor's special relationship with government is a decidedly mixed blessing. The following statement of an Ensenada labor leader could also stand as a comment on the situation in Jalapa: "The government has to give in to some of the demands of the labor groups in the same way that the labor groups have to give in to some of the demands of the government . . . when the government asks for support in some political matter, or for backing for some of the candidates. . . . Of necessity the labor federations have to back the government, otherwise at the hour we need help from the government they would screw us."[10]

The students of the University of Veracruz represent an unusual group in the municipio. They are on the whole significantly less interested in obtaining specific benefits for themselves than either business or labor. They thus loom as a "free" element, attracted to issues and causes in a way not otherwise common in the city. As a consequence, they are often seen as the only source of serious criticism of the regime and of government policies. Political leaders sometimes mentioned in interviews that they especially fear student participation because of its unpredictability and capacity for disruption. Various factors combine to permit students unusual latitude in political expression: They are relatively immune to the kinds of reprisals that threaten the livelihoods of businessmen and workers; they are unusually articulate and able to communicate and organize quickly among themselves; and they benefit from a traditional tolerance for student

[10] Ugalde, *Power and Conflict*, p. 42.

political activism and dissent.[11] Furthermore, at least at the University of Veracruz, there is a student subculture that encourages and supports political involvement outside the university. Above all, many students perceive and are offended by the gap between democratic rhetoric and expectations on the one hand and the realities of the essentially closed governmental apparatus on the other.[12]

During 1966, with the exception of a protest demonstration over United States policy in Vietnam (not a threat to local authorities), there was, however, only one occasion on which large numbers of students were especially active in Jalapa. Heavy trucks traveling through the city had been barred from the central streets and required by the state traffic authorities to use an unpaved bypass route. But in June that route was nearly impassable because of heavy seasonal rains. A truck drivers' union appealed to the university students for help and together they created a fairly large though peaceful street demonstration in front of the state capital. Jalapa's *El Diario* for June 29, 1966, identified the participating students as representing the Student Federation and organizations in the Schools of Law, Economics, Business, and Architecture, and as from the preparatory schools. Perhaps even more impressive was a traffic stoppage at both main entrances to the city. Dozens of trucks parked on the highways, completely blocking traffic for about four hours. A delegation of truckers and students went to see "the man"— meaning, of course, the governor. He told them that as far as the state was concerned it would be an even greater injustice to permit heavy trucks on the city thoroughfares. Such traffic, he said, would soon destroy the pavement constructed at great cost to the state and "the people of Veracruz." Because the bypass was

[11] That tolerance proved fragile when government forces in Mexico City killed dozens and imprisoned many more students just prior to the 1968 Olympic Games. The killings in Mexico City precipitated large student protest demonstrations in Jalapa. The Governor responded by jailing many students and some faculty members, but considerable pressure arose within the community, and the Jalapa prisoners were released a few days later.

[12] For additional information, see William Tuohy and Barry Ames, *Mexican University Students in Politics: Rebels Without Allies?* Monograph Series in World Affairs, 7.3 (University of Denver, 1970).

maintained by a federal agency, the governor suggested that the students and truckers present their case to the Ministry of Public Works. Thus, redirected if not satisfied, they left the state offices. As an immediate response from the federal agency there was an emergency road-grading effort, and slightly over a year later, a more satisfactory bypass surface was built. From the students' viewpoint, a satisfactory demonstration of solidarity with the workers had been made, reputations had been enhanced, and an image of selflessness had been reinforced. The truckers were less impressed with the immediate outcome, but unable to do more.

Finally, it would seem that the Church as an organized interest group is not very active in politics.[13] Churchmen are, of course, concerned with public affairs, but because of the considerable anticlericalism in Mexico they must behave circumspectly and intervene, if at all, indirectly. Remembrance of past Church influence still colors some informants' perceptions of its present role ("the Church is not politically strong in Jalapa, but it never gives up trying"), but there is substantial agreement that churchmen do not constitute a group in the same sense that labor, business, and students do. In similar fashion, the Order of Masons (La Logia Masónica) has largely retreated from its once-active political role. Our most knowledgeable informant on the subject (an active Mason) said that six lodges, each with about thirty members, were active in the city. These lodges stand ready to oppose clerical intervention in public affairs and they certainly provide a meeting ground for men interested in political contacts and promoting their careers.[14] Thus, like the Church,

[13] However, since 95 percent of our respondents thought of themselves as Catholics (and of these, 90 percent said they attended church once a month or oftener), the Church cannot be ignored. It is undoubtedly important in reinforcing or conditioning politically relevant attitudes and behaviors. But the fact that the most active religious following is predominantly female detracts from the secular importance and influence of the priesthood. Moreover, frequency of church attendance is not independently related to the social and political orientations discussed in Chapters 4 and 5. Thus it would be misleading to infer political positions directly from intensity of religious identification.

[14] A Jalapan saying holds, "No todos los masones son bribones, pero todos los bribones pretenden ser masones" (Not all Masons are scoundrels, but all scoundrels aspire to be Masons).

they are part of the larger environment in which government and interest groups interact, but they are not themselves a particularly active organization.

Responses, Non-Responses, and Conflict

Large-scale government involvement in the daily life of the community means that a wide variety of interests come to be defined as politically relevant and are thus communicated as high in the official hierarchy as their advocates can reach. The initial treatment of those demands illuminates yet another feature of municipal politics, for those who man Jalapa's local political institutions usually are neither motivated nor able to combine demands into general policy alternatives. State government is consequently besieged with unaggregated requests, many presented to it directly, others coming only after unsatisfactory responses at the community level.

Although the municipal PRI and the ayuntamiento might seem to be natural arenas for bringing together demands, in fact they do not as a rule perform that function. Like other community organizations that occasionally synthesize interests and present their consensus as a claim on higher levels of government (the Chamber of Commerce, the Rotary Club, the Lions Club, and various *ad hoc* committees), the local PRI and ayuntamiento operate only in relation to a limited range of topics. Specifically, local PRI officers respond primarily to government initiatives, and thus neither propose policy nor seriously mediate conflicting program proposals. Even questions that are nominally of internal Party concern tend to be communicated directly to the state leadership rather than resolved within the local PRI hierarchy. On the other hand, ayuntamiento authorities actually discourage the aggregation of claims by approaching community problems with narrow perspectives in terms of both time and technique. Thus, bundles of separate demands that cannot simply be ignored or set aside at lower levels eventually get passed on to higher authorities to be handled in piecemeal and often unpredictable fashion.

The confusion and inaction occasioned by this fragmented competition for attention and resources are further complicated by the absence of developmental planning of the sort that might provide criteria for evaluating claims on scarce resources. There is not, for example, a city plan for regulating public and private construction projects and controlling and organizing land use. This means that there are no formally established guidelines by which needs are appraised or specific undertakings such as street development projects are assigned to the ayuntamiento, the Junta de Mejoramiento, or the state. For almost a decade there has been a state law outlining the goals and general administrative organization of urban planning for the cities of Veracruz. A second state law applies just to Jalapa, but it too is very general. Detailed regulations and provisions for enforcement are supposed to be established by the ayuntamiento, but successive administrations have done little or nothing in this realm. Of the considerable information about community life and facilities that would be required to formulate a thorough plan, only part has even been collected: existing data relate mostly to property usage and traffic patterns, neglecting almost all important socio-economic concerns. So far in Jalapa, only a few stabs at "planning for a plan," calling upon the State Planning Commission and local architects and engineers for assistance, have been made. When questioned about these matters, the mayor replied, "Steps are being taken to make planning possible."

In Jalapa as elsewhere, these "steps" may be more meaningfully interpreted as delaying tactics rather than as the beginnings of substantive progress. Why should this be the case? In part because members of the ayuntamiento seem to take their short tenure in office as a reason not to act in the realm of planning. It is a realm in which activity brings no immediate career rewards and is moreover almost certain to engender divisive conflicts, at least in the short run. Furthermore, there is a conviction among many of the technicians involved—architects and engineers who have worked with municipal government—that ayuntamiento members neither understand the basic problems and their technical manifestations nor care to learn. Moreover, there is widespread feeling that rational planning is subverted by the incessant operation of personalism. As expressed by a labor official and ex-member of the ayuntamiento, "Unfortunately, those municipal projects are done because *el señor diputado* lives on that street and it must be fixed; because *el señor general* lives in that neighborhood, is bothered by the noise, and something has to be done; and it is necessary to fix that other street because the aunt of *el señor diputado* lives there." Additionally, major alterations in existing physical arrangements are seen as prohibitively costly not only by government but also by the relevant sectors of the public themselves.

Municipal inaction and non-response due to lack of money and lack of planning are both cause and consequence of the political impoverishment of local institutions. This can be seen most clearly in the recruitment and subsequent behavior of local officials. The lack of resources, status, and leadership opportunities in municipal politics combines with the physical proximity of the state political apparatus to drain talent away from community structures and toward the state and even the federal levels. Political and bureaucratic leftovers predominate among local officials, along with some citizens "not regularly in politics" who tend to be naive about most political affairs. As a rule, local incumbents mingle neither politically nor socially with the *hermandad política*, the sometimes cut-throat circle of hard-driving políticos who have made it or are clearly on the way up in state politics. Moreover, selection of ayuntamiento officials ignores most relevant professional qualifications, further weakening that body. Even in the case of the presidente municipal, as one ex-mayor explained in an interview, the PRI nominee often is a man who "never has administered anything." Such inexperience is usually still more pronounced among the regidores and síndicos.

The recruitment process has another unfortunate correlate, revealed in the comment of an ex-mayor who when interviewed said, "Quite simply, the ayuntamiento is not composed of men elected by the people, but rather by men placed in office by a political party. These officials have no commitment to the people." Local officials owe their selection to the governor, to the PRI, or to an organization such as a trade union. The short, three-year term of office also detracts from an ayuntamiento's collective sense of responsibility, for officials are in office only briefly and cannot be held accountable in the next election. Chosen as a reward for prior service and guaranteed election, left almost without resources and knowing that they will not have to answer for their performance in office, local officials are thus only occasionally at the service of the community. At the municipio level, political irresponsibility and limited responsiveness are thus inseparable from powerlessness, centralism, and careerism.[15]

Despite the lack of planning and the political impoverishment of local institutions, there are many occasions on which projects involving citizen cooperation do get undertaken and completed smoothly and successfully. Thus, before examining in more detail some examples of conflict between government and citizens, we will briefly sketch a project that ran without undue delay or difficulties.

Calle Francisco Madero. The need for new pavement, sidewalks, and better drainage facilities on Madero Street had long been apparent and had repeatedly been sought by its residents. But no major improvements had been made, the ayuntamiento always pleading lack of money and more urgent needs elsewhere.

---

[15] At this point a word about corruption seems in order. Small payments to petty officials for services rendered are so common that Mexican slang has a word for them—*la mordida* (the bite). Such transactions have long been considered unavoidable special arrangements or semi-justifiable supplements to low salaries rather than criminal acts. But when higher-level officials receive property or payments for favoritism, that passes into the domain of corruption. Such high-level misbehavior, obviously difficult to document in any case, is probably not very extensive in the ayuntamiento of Jalapa. Resources are severely limited and officials closely supervised. Stories of corruption in the state government abound, particularly among students, but in the absence of a muckraking press and crusading politicians, one can only speculate about such things as the considerable wealth accumulated by former governors.

Then, early in 1964, at a time when no such request was before him, the mayor decided that improvements were aesthetically and politically desirable. Madero Street was, after all, located close to *el centro* and in a section that had historical value as one of the oldest parts of the city. He also stressed the obvious benefits to the residents. The ayuntamiento's staff architect was instructed to draw up technical plans, make cost estimates, and calculate the share that would be owed by each property owner. Simultaneously, ayuntamiento officials began contacting the street's residents in their homes, by mail, and in neighborhood meetings, to see whether they were willing and able to share in the construction costs.

Roughly one month after his decision to undertake the project, the mayor had before him the plans (including detailed cost projections and the breakdown by property frontage), expressions of public interest, and official estimates of each property owner's ability to contribute. Construction could begin as soon as the mayor decided how the costs were to be shared by the municipality and the owners as a group, and as soon as individuals' frontage-based allotments were adjusted according to their capacity to pay. The mayor decided that the city could and, in view of the neighborhood's economic status, would probably have to pay 50 percent of the total cost of 110,000 pesos (8,800 dollars). The street's residents were then contacted again, and each signed a promissory note for an agreed-upon share, with payments spread over five years. Initially all expenses were covered by the ayuntamiento as the financing agent. A formal announcement was made, and the work was completed by municipal employees within a few months. There were subsequently no serious collection difficulties.

As has previously been suggested, overt conflict between government and citizens is in danger of erupting not when officials fail to act in response to outstanding public needs or demands but rather when they make an unpopular or arbitrary decision and thus create or collide with a recalcitrant sector of the public. This is what happened when Jalapa's streets were closed to trucks and the students sided with the truckers in a public dem-

onstration of protest. Certainly the possibility of encountering
an uncooperative group of property owners on Madero Street
was very much on officials' minds when they were bargaining
with the residents. Through careful groundwork and consideration of the limits of popular support, they neutralized the possible opposition. On other occasions, however, potentially recalcitrant groups are not handled so successfully; officials are then
faced with delicate, embarrassing, and sometimes costly situations. Another street improvement project and a local tax controversy illustrate how such situations are generated and how
they are usually resolved.

Avenida Venustiano Carranza. Carranza Avenue is a major
thoroughfare in the southern part of Jalapa, cutting through a
mixed though predominantly lower-middle-class neighborhood.
For many years its condition had varied from bad to mediocre
as only occasional and partial repairs were made. Broken pavement and periodic flooding into adjacent homes brought recurring complaints from both residents and users, but not until 1964
was the problem attacked in a comprehensive manner. That
year, with no particular advance notice or exceptional public
demand, Governor Fernando López Arias decided that work
was urgently needed. At his instruction the local Junta de Mejoramiento, in collaboration with the State Department of Communications and Public Works, quickly made the necessary technical studies. The Governor decided that construction should
proceed at once, and the state then instructed the local Junta
to arrange payment of the total cost by property owners on the
Avenue, dividing the assessment according to frontage as was
customary.

The state government considered the work too urgent to await
the completion of financial agreements with property owners;
thus the Junta was directed to let contracts to private companies,
and work crews were actually on the scene before public support had been organized or financial contributions agreed upon.
When Junta representatives contacted the citizens involved and
asked them to cover the total cost of the work, opposition arose

immediately. Organized informally among neighbors, resistance focused on the arbitrariness of the decision to undertake the project and on the high cost of the work. As a thoroughfare, Carranza Avenue required more costly improvements than streets restricted to local traffic. Furthermore it is not clear whether money was saved or lost in letting the contract to private firms. Construction was already under way when the property owners formally refused to sign promissory notes, thereby not only placing the financing of the project in doubt, but acutely embarrassing the Junta in its role of collection agency for the state.

The dispute was temporarily resolved when the state agreed to negotiate the issue with property owners through the local Junta. Subsequently state officials relented in their demands that property owners pay the total cost. Costs were to be shared, with a proprietor's contribution based on frontage and adjusted in instances of financial hardship. When notes were finally signed, citizens were scheduled to pay 35 percent of the total cost of 485,000 pesos (38,800 dollars) with the state assuming the rest.[16] Even at that moment, however, some observers predicted that they would never be paid because the project had cost so much, had caused so much ill will, and because the property owners thought the Junta could not and the state would not compel payment in the face of widespread resistance. That prediction has proven relatively accurate: two years later we find the Junta appealing publicly—and apparently without success—for payment.

Tax Boycott of 1966. Late in 1965, after the state had increased its property tax rate, the ayuntamiento doubled its tax on residential property from three to six pesos per thousand of assessed

[16] These figures were provided by the Office of the State Coordinator of Juntas de Mejoramiento, which also provide detailed breakdowns by property owner. As an indication of the scale of this project and the inability of the municipio to undertake works of this magnitude, the 485,000 pesos to be paid by the state and private citizens exceeded the total amount in the discretionary public works fund of the ayuntamiento budget for 1964.

valuation. This increase was clearly legal under a state law allowing municipios to set rates as high as 150 percent of the prevailing state rate on the same type of property. Vocal opposition to the proposed increase broke out, organized principally by a homeowners' association, the Unión de Propietarios de Fincas Rústicas y Urbanas. Members of that association and other property owners then boycotted the controversial tax. After twenty days of the "strike," in January 1966, the ayuntamiento relented and rescinded the increase.

Neither politically nor economically could the ayuntamiento long endure the tax boycott. The association claimed 3,000 members primarily in the lower middle class, representing 7,000 properties. Other informants, although more cautious in estimating the association's membership, cited figures of up to 20 percent of the homeowners in Jalapa. With sympathetic nonmembers also withholding payments, the boycott deprived the municipality of badly needed revenues, for the tax on urban residential properties is the second largest single source (usually about one-sixth) of ayuntamiento income. Local officials were also deeply troubled politically, embarrassed by their ineffectiveness in the face of "illegal" opposition, and essentially without recourse when it became apparent that the state government would not intervene to enforce the new tax rate.

Tax-related controversies can erupt even when there is no clear assessment of "new" taxes. For example, a public street-cleaning service had been instituted in the mid-1950's under a system whereby contributions by householders paid the entire cost. Clearly voluntary at the outset, these contributions had come to be regarded by officials as mandatory payments for services rendered. During the summer of 1966, however, residents of some neighborhoods challenged the ayuntamiento's right to impose the monthly fee of 15 pesos per household. They charged that the fee not only was excessive but constituted an illegal tax, and they subsequently refused to pay. The ayuntamiento denied both assertions. Each side claimed legal justification in the same two state laws, The Law of Municipal Finance

(*Ley de Hacienda Municipal*) and the Law of Municipal Revenue (*Ley de Ingresos Municipales*), neither of which, however,
specifically mentioned payment for such service. The only resolution reached by the end of the summer was the suspension of
service in the non-paying neighborhoods. Although the state
government could have intervened (with a definitive legal statement, for example), in accordance with its hands-off posture in
sensitive yet non-critical local matters, it did not choose to do so.

Aggravated by a limited industrial tax base, the revenue situation in Jalapa is a microcosm of tax assessment and collection
problems in Mexico. Citizens seem to expect substantial government services even as they express cynicism about the honesty
and competence of those who are supposed to provide the services. The government tries hard to tax the actual recipients of
services, and the recipients try just as hard to escape such focused taxes. Taxable commercial transactions often go unreport-
ed, thereby increasing the proportion of revenues that must come
from other sources. Everyone is suspicious, for, in the words of
one federal official, "the businessman always feels robbed and
the government always feels cheated." In sum, government, particularly at the local level, is susceptible to pressures and strate-
gies aimed at reducing, deferring, or escaping taxes, and it is precisely local government that has the fewest contingency funds to
fall back on when collection becomes difficult or impossible. In
such environments, raising taxes enough to improve services
measurably does not seem a viable alternative. Rather, to try
to raise taxes is to bring into the public arena all the contradictory and clashing forces and beliefs that abound in the community, and then to risk failure and embarrassment. In Jalapa, as
elsewhere in Mexico, a more generous gathering and a more rational disbursement of public monies will not come easily.

The Citizen Agenda: Problems and Possibilities

To this point it has been argued that despite a multiplicity of
claims on government it is not usually the rejection of specific
demands that occasions community conflict but arbitrary, ill-

prepared, and consequently unpopular attempts to raise general revenue or collect funds for local improvements. (As we shall see in more detail in Chapter 5, widespread distrust of both the motives and the capabilities of politicians and administrators deeply conditions these moments of conflict, for people give money to government projects only grudgingly, even when direct benefits are promised.) Just because overt community conflict is thus limited, however, we should not assume that at other times Jalapeños are indifferent to urban problems. If they do not get together to press claims on government or march through *el centro* demanding jobs, electrification, better drainage, or adequate public transportation, it is not because they fail to view these as problems or are unaffected by them. There *is* an agenda of citizen concerns, but because these concerns are fragmented and unorganized, and because the distribution of resources and the political culture in Jalapa are not conducive to translating them into public issues, the political system remains relatively unaffected. Although a fuller understanding of why the agenda remains so private (i.e., isolated from public life) will have to await the analyses of Chapters 4 and 5, its substance can be presented here.

Very early in our general interviews with citizens we asked, "What, in your opinion, are the most urgent or serious problems that affect Jalapa?" Responses to that question, broken down by sex, are presented in Table 3.3. What is striking about these data is how completely the economic and service themes dominate. If complaints about the cost of living are thought of as a special way of expressing dissatisfaction with the economic situation, then 46 percent of all respondents feel that jobs, salaries, and living costs are the city's primary problem. If lack of other urban services and insufficiencies in schools are added to complaints about drainage, pavement, water, and electricity, then 47 percent of all respondents single out local services as the city's primary problem. Living as they do with the daily inconvenience of poor and often muddy streets, lack of water, and other shortages, it is not surprising that women more often than

TABLE 3.3

What Are the Most Serious Problems of Jalapa?
(*Percent of Responses by Sex*)

Problem	Men (N = 738)	Women (N = 671)	Combined (N = 1,409)
Economic situation: shortage of work, unemployment, lack of industry, low salaries, etc.	52%	26%	39%
Drainage and pavement: lack of sewers, unpaved streets, need for street repairs, etc.	21	43	32
Lack of water and/or electricity: water stops, poor service, have to carry water, no electricity, etc.	6	8	7
Cost of living: high rents, food expensive, homes too expensive, basics cost too much, etc.	3	11	7
Lack of other urban services: infrequent and dirty buses, poor police protection, etc.	5	4	4
Insufficiencies in schools: shortage of schools, poor teachers, etc.	4	3	4
Lack of justice; immorality: government unjust, abuses of authority, decline in morality	4	1	3
Taxes: high taxes, too many taxes, high cost of public services (tax-related), etc.	2	1	1
Other: lack of land, deforestation, mistreatment of the young, etc.	3	3	3
TOTAL	100%	100%	100%

NOTE: Since only 5 percent of all respondents mentioned more than one problem, multiple responses have not been tabulated. Because of non-responses and missing data, the total *N*'s reported in this and subsequent tables are usually less than 1,556.

men mention lack of these services. On the other hand, since it is usually men who experience the difficulties and humiliations of the labor market, they more often mention the general economic situation—although the impact of that situation on women as managers of the home does show up in their more frequent mentions of the cost of living.

What Table 3.3 does not show is that the frequency with which problems are mentioned does not vary greatly by social class. As might be expected, there are some differences—the middle class most often mentions cost of living, the upper class more often mentions lack of urban services *other than* drainage, pavement, water, and electricity—but the overall impression is one of a common vocabulary of problems.[17] It should be emphasized that this common vocabulary inevitably masks a great objective diversity of life experiences. The rich man's concern with the economic semi-stagnation of Jalapa is not the same as the poor man's, nor is the middle-class housewife's complaint about impure or inadequate water the same as the poor housewife's complaint about no household water supply at all. Nevertheless, Jalapeños share the common experience of living together in a city in which jobs and services are both in short supply. And although these shortages impinge very differently on people from different social and economic strata, almost all citizens would agree on this basic, two-item agenda.

Equally impressive is the near unanimity (91 percent of our sample) with which Jalapeños feel themselves powerless to do anything about the problem they would place at the top of the agenda. Instead, most of them (87 percent), when asked who has the responsibility for solving this problem, say "The government." About a third specifically referred to the state government, about a fifth either to the federal or to the local government, and the rest simply to "el gobierno."[18]

Paradoxically, Jalapeños are almost as quick to denigrate politicians and official procedures as they are to dump their agenda of problems into the government's lap. And to compound the

[17] The one important sex-related exception to this generalization is the frequency with which women mention the economic situation. Only 15 percent of upper-class women say it is the city's most important problem, whereas 20 percent of middle-class women and 34 percent of lower-class women do so.

[18] Responses of "el gobierno" usually do not conceal a direct reference to local government, for the latter is not commonly spoken of as *el gobierno* but rather as *el ayuntamiento* or *el municipio*. Only 4 percent of the respondents singled out businessmen or private industry as having primary responsibility. Among the scattered remaining responses (9 percent) were many that actually referred indirectly to government through the mention of a specific bureaucracy considered responsible for inadequate services or facilities.

paradox, in spite of these negative orientations toward politics, they give little attention to "good government"—or the lack of it—on their list of the community's problems.[19]

The local agenda is singlemindedly focused on economic and service deficiencies to the almost complete exclusion of structural and political problems. It is an agenda of people who live in a well managed political environment—one in which conflict is limited to occasional tax and service issues that get out of hand. Above all, it is the agenda of a citizenry that has not made the connection between private troubles and public objects except to identify government as responsible for helping out. Missing is a sense that the political process could be other than it is, that politics might be part of the problem, or that change in the basic economic situation implies change in the political system as well. Although visions of a city in which the economic situation is not so harsh and services of all kinds are more plentiful are clearly implied by the agenda, no such image of either the possibility or the necessity of an improved political process is suggested. It is an agenda to warm the heart of the most complacent public official, for nowhere therein would he find the germ of a challenge to business-as-usual in party, bureaucracy, or government.

In the short run, it is clear that effective, community-wide responses to the items on the agenda are far beyond the fiscal and administrative capabilities of the ayuntamiento. Even the state government—given the multiplicity of demands on its resources —could meet Jalapa's more pressing needs only through rank favoritism or the neglect of other developmental projects. The government's helplessness to respond in other than piecemeal and particularistic ways is to an extent understood by Jalapeños and, as we shall see in Chapter 5, government is forgiven as well as disparaged for its incapacity to perform.

[19] University students living in Jalapa (a group that is more "political" than the population in general) differ sharply from our overall adult sample in this respect. About 12 percent of the students interviewed listed government shortcomings as the city's most important problem (a figure that rose to almost a third when multiple responses were counted). See Tuohy and Ames, pp. 17, 21.

Equally realistic though different conclusions were arrived at several decades ago when the architects of Mexico's civic order recognized that state and local authorities working alone could never provide the economic opportunities and services that would be needed in the urban areas. The help of the private sector, both those who commanded major talents and resources and those of more modest means, would be required. It was precisely to evoke these private resources and to coordinate their use in developmental projects that the Juntas de Mejoramiento, Moral, Cívico, y Material were created. Yet ultimately the mechanism of the Junta also proved disappointing as both leaders and citizens came to see its flaws and reinforce its failings through their own perceptions and behavior. The genesis, flowering, and subsequent degeneration of the Jalapa Junta may serve as an example. For although this Junta may have expanded more rapidly, performed more effectively, and collapsed more precipitously than most, the sources of its failures are fairly typical. Above all, its history illuminates the difficulties of mounting a community-wide, self-sustaining attack on local problems. It is thus a fitting episode with which to end this chapter.

Jalapa's Junta was one of the first in what later became a statewide and then a nationwide pattern of such organizations during the presidency of Adolfo Ruiz Cortines (1952–58). As Governor of Veracruz in 1945, Ruiz Cortines had given official recognition to a previously informal Jalapeño group with the announced goal of regularizing and increasing the participation of private citizens in community development. This Junta, like others that were then being formed, was to be a nongovernmental board that would assist and promote private initiative in response to community problems and needs, thus acting as a "nonpartisan" bridge between the public and the private sector, particularly the more affluent businessmen in the latter.

The Junta gradually came to play an important role in Jalapa. Its influence grew steadily during the late 1940's and was at a peak in the mid-1950's. In those years the Junta sponsored numerous street and drainage construction projects, instigated construction of a road to a nearby city, publicized local tourist attractions, and actively solicited federal support of various other community projects. The costs of these public works were in large part defrayed by substantial federal subsidies—millions of pesos, according to usually reliable informants—that flowed directly to the local Junta, actually giving it far more money than the ayuntamiento had in those years. The ultimate source of that uncommon flow of funds was President Ruiz Cortines himself; he not only had a continuing interest in his creation, the local Junta, but was following a Mexican tradition whereby an incumbent president's native state receives extraordinary federal benefits. In fact, Ruiz Cortines had already elicited special favors for Veracruz and Jalapa from his predecessor, President Miguel Alemán (1946–52), also a native of the state.

Although material resources were clearly fundamental, the nature of the organization's leadership during the 1950's is also important in understanding the success of the Junta. From its inception through 1962 the Junta was made up of some of Jalapa's most prestigious citizens from business, the professions, and the government bureaucracy. Lawyers, doctors, engineers, businessmen, and bureaucrats brought vital technical and political skills to Junta affairs. Many were also personally acquainted with President Ruiz Cortines, a number having served with him in the state government. Undoubtedly the most prominent Junta member, and its president during the period of greatest activity, was Justo Fernández, a nationally known and very successful businessman from Jalapa. In addition to Don Justo's political connections (including family ties to ex-President Avila Camacho) his local status gave him ready access to all segments of the community including the otherwise often recalcitrant business sector. He was an ideal broker—politically and economically well connected, respected and trusted by others in the community. Furthermore, the way in which members of the Junta were selected lent it an air of legitimacy. They were chosen for indefinite terms through a semi-popular recruitment process in which nominations submitted by various community organizations were voted on by representatives of the organizations and other prominent citizens. Apparently there was a continuing sense of public participation, with considerable citizen interest and even some competition for posts. The organization was hardly democratic, but it did realistically represent powerful groups and interests in the community.

The period of the Junta's greatest activity and political autonomy came to an end in 1958, when Ruiz Cortines left the Presidency and major federal subsidies were terminated. Loss of that extraordinary support would have been sufficient in itself sharply to curtail Junta operations; another blow was the departure of Justo Fernández who, although nominally on the board through 1962, moved away from Jalapa in the late 1950's and withdrew from community affairs. Together, these changes deprived the Junta of both money and influence just when it was beginning to face its toughest projects, those located in the outlying areas of the city where needs were greatest and propertyowners were least able to contribute to improvements.

A major threat to the autonomy of the Junta had already appeared in 1957 when newly inaugurated Governor Quirasco created the office of State Coordinator of Juntas de Mejoramiento. Whether that move was prompted by jealousy of the Jalapa Junta's power and prominence (as alleged by one informant) or whether it represented a genuine effort to improve the coordination of projects on a statewide basis, it certainly signaled the beginning of the end for the rare amalgam of officials and private citizens who had been so effective in obtaining benefits for the city and eliciting cooperation and contributions from its more affluent citizens. Soon after the inauguration of Governor López Arias in 1962, the men who had been on the Junta through the 1950's resigned, explaining that they had served long enough and emphasizing the incoming governor's right to fill public offices. Junta positions had not traditionally been considered part of the patronage at the governor's disposal, but sensing that the Junta they had known was already doomed to impotency because of the cutting off of federal funds, its members in effect consigned its remains to the state authorities.

Under López Arias (1962–68) the state government intervened directly in most Junta affairs. Only a voluntary contribution by local coffee processors kept the small bureaucracy together, and the unpaid board shrank to a third of its former size. The elitist but nevertheless well legitimated mechanisms of community recruitment fell into disuse, and new board members were in essence appointed by the state government, acting through the State Coordinator's office. As a result, the board came to be the province of men of considerably less prestige and personal resources than before.[20]

Legal control over the Junta's operations was also extended.[21] These changes, which took place in 1962 and 1963, were described by a former Junta leader as follows: "The administrative position of the Junta was changed. Formerly, we were working under a state law that did no more than require a reporting of the Junta's projects, expenditures, etc. Now, the Junta is directly controlled by an office of the state government. . . . It appears that the members of the Junta who succeeded us were less enthusiastic, or lacked the same social and political resources or whatever else is necessary. . . . In a body like this it is crucial for

[20] The board that served from the mid-1950's through 1962 had 22 members; its president was Justo Fernández and its vice-president was Dr. Miguel Dorantes. Members came from business, government bureaucracy, and the professions, roughly distributed as follows: one medical doctor and sometime administrator of government hospitals, seven businessmen or industrialists, four men who held both business and government or education posts, seven exclusively in government jobs (state and federal), and three teachers. Identifiable professional credentials were those of one doctor, three engineers, four lawyers, two architects, four teachers/professors, and one economist. By contrast, the 1966 Junta had only six members: three businessmen, one labor leader, and one teacher/professor, and one state government bureaucrat. The only professional credentials represented were those of the teacher and an engineer (the bureaucrat). The names of Junta members were supplied by the Jalapa office staff; occupations and professions were identified with the aid of that staff and of informants acquainted with the men involved.

[21] Illustrative of some of the legal controls introduced are requirements that all Juntas in the state formulate and get prior approval from the governor for an annual program of works and obey instructions given by the governor and by the State Coordinator's office. The governor also is empowered to remove any Junta member and then either appoint a replacement or call an election meeting (*Estado de Veracruz, Ley de Juntas de Mejoramiento Moral, Cívico, y Material,* 1963).

the members to have many contacts." By then virtually inactive and subordinate to state authorities, the Junta came to be, in the words of one prominent citizen and informant, "a mere collector for the state." It was in this capacity that the Junta operated (albeit not very successfully) when Carranza Avenue was improved.[22]

Shifts in attitudes among both the public and Junta members have accompanied the loss of political and fiscal autonomy. For many citizens the Junta is now just one more governmental agency, to be approached in the same spirit as other agencies when seeking aid and to be avoided on other occasions for much the same reasons. This identification with the government destroys the catalytic and creative role the Junta was supposed to play: it cannot now evoke from the business community or the citizenry at large the extra resources and the extra measure of cooperation denied to official agencies. There is a general feeling, reinforced by the arbitrary way in which public works projects are selected, that initiatives from citizens are not rewarded, and that it is best to remain passive. As one Junta incumbent explained when interviewed, "The basic problem is one of attitude—everybody waits for the government to do whatever needs to be done. If the problem or need becomes sufficiently acute, they know that sooner or later the government will handle it." Although this attitude is not, as this informant claimed, the basic problem, but only one of its symptoms, the characterization of the community as now essentially passive seems accurate. The capacity of either public or private institutions to transform pride in the community and local and national connections into material benefits for the citizens is thus much reduced from the days when Don Justo and the Junta were at the peak of their effectiveness.

In retrospect, it is obvious that the successes of the Junta

[22] At the same time, state government displeasure with Junta inactivity had never been greater. For example, in 1966 the State Coordinator of Juntas de Mejoramiento "called upon the members of the Junta . . . of Jalapa to avoid restricting their activities to purely administrative questions and extend their efforts to actively promoting works for the public welfare." *El Tiempo* (Jalapa), Aug. 31, 1966.

were somewhat artificial. Extraordinary federal subsidies, personal contacts with the President, freedom from state control, and talented and vigorous leadership were not normal conditions, nor could they be expected to continue indefinitely. Scarcity and centralized control returned, and interest waned. The relationship between strong and resourceful leadership and extraordinary resources was positive and self-reinforcing. But when the resources disappeared, the leaders moved on to other public arenas or returned to more private styles of life. It would be a mistake, however, to view the retired Junta leadership as merely the elicitors, guardians, and dispensors of federal largesse. They were also able to call forth money, talent, and cooperation from the community. Thus, an elitist civic subculture grew up under the protective shelter provided by federal monies and attention. It was a fragile and dependent growth, however, and once the shelter was removed, the harsh light of state and municipal realities caused it to wither and die.

Finally, it should be emphasized that the existence of the Junta as an institution, whether weak or strong, implies a criticism of government, particularly municipal government. The Junta is a legally sanctioned manifestation of lack of confidence in the ayuntamiento. This is not lost on ayuntamiento members, who take every opportunity to reaffirm themselves as constitutionally the highest and only true local authorities. But this self-image of the ayuntamiento is not universally accepted, and many community leaders continue to believe that the Junta idea is still relevant and will remain so as long as municipal government is impoverished, unrepresentative, unresponsive, and unimaginative.

Four

Inequality, Advantage, and the Status Quo

Jalapa is home to many different kinds of people. Lawyers, bureaucrats, clerks, laborers, peddlers, shoeshine boys, school children, housewives, domestics, all crowd into the city's streets and public places. The human geography of the city can be mapped as richly and in as much detail as the observer—be he poet or sociologist—wishes. For our purposes, however, an understanding of the basic social structure of Jalapa must take precedence over an appreciation of the variety of individual personalities and life-styles to be found there.

Work, Money, and School

Of the several common ways to locate individuals in the social structure, rankings by occupation, income, and education are the most frequently used. Additionally, the relative number of persons holding certain kinds of jobs or receiving certain levels of income is commonly taken as indicative of the overall character of a city or society. Thus, we speak of "industrial" cities when many workers are employed in factories, or of "hard-core" poverty in a society when a certain percentage of families have incomes below some agreed-upon minimum. Such characterizations are, of course, always based on comparisons—implied or explicit—with other cities, societies, or ideal types.

The distribution of occupations in Jalapa clearly reflects its

TABLE 4.1

*Occupational Distribution of the Adult Population
of Jalapa*

Occupation	Percent including housewives $(N = 1,470)^a$	Percent excluding housewives $(N = 906)$
Professional, executive, managerial	7%	12%
Clerical or sales	11	18
Small business	11	17
Skilled labor	14	22
Manual labor	10	17
Domestic service	4	6
Farming or farm work	5	8
Housewife	38	—
TOTAL	100%	100%

a Eighty-four students, the retired, the unemployed, and people who did not reply are excluded. Respondents were encouraged to state their usual occupation; thus the actual number of unemployed is probably understated through the inclusion in the total *N* of those who considered themselves "between jobs" (temporarily unemployed).

bureaucratic and commercial character.[1] As Table 4.1 shows, once housewives are removed from the sample, those in business, clerical, sales, and professional occupations almost equal the number holding manual occupations. Of course, to be a small businessman may mean to peddle *tortas* and thus to have less income and less status than a skilled worker; but even allowing for such situations, the commercial and white-collar presence in Jalapa is impressive.

Data on monthly family income, however, caution against inferring any widespread degree of creature comfort and material affluence from this occupational picture. As can be seen in Table 4.2, a third of all respondents say that their monthly family income is less than 500 pesos ($40), and almost another third report an income of only $40 to $80 a month. Although the median

[1] Appendix A compares the Jalapan distribution with estimates for urban Mexico in general. As an example of occupational skewness in Jalapa, 12 percent of our respondents report professional or executive occupations, as opposed to an estimate of just over 5 percent for all of urban Mexico.

TABLE 4.2

Reported Monthly Family Income of Respondents

Income range (pesos)	Percent of respondents (N = 1,416)
Less than 500 ($40)	33%
500–999 ($40–80)	30
1,000–1,999 ($80–160)	20
2,000–2,999 ($160–240)	8
3,000–3,999 ($240–320)	5
4,000–5,999 ($320–480)	3
6,000 or more ($480 or more)	1
TOTAL	100%

NOTE: The local minimum wage in Jalapa in 1966 was 21.5 pesos a day or approximately 500 pesos a month. The minimum wage, however, is not applicable to all jobs, and it frequently is not enforced.

family income of between $60 and $70 a month sets Jalapans well apart from their impoverished rural countrymen, it does not leave the average family with either a sense of financial security or the capacity to indulge most of the consumer aspirations generated in the contemporary Mexican urban setting. In fact, the bureaucratic, commercial, and white-collar cast of the city should not be thought to imply even relative prosperity. Jalapa is no boom town. Most wage-earning citizens, including those who have "respectable" middle-class jobs, receive modest salaries and perforce live simply. Although they may be tantalized by dreams of a life-style that includes new kitchen appliances, private schools for the children, or a more elegant wardrobe, such dreams are only fantasies on $70 a month. In reality they count centavos and make sure their roomers don't leave the lights burning.

Equally modest are the educational achievements of most Jalapeños. Over half of all respondents report that they either never attended school at all (16 percent) or did not complete primary school (sixth grade; 38 percent). Another 21 percent finished primary school, but went no further. Thus, three out of four adults have had no secondary schooling, and most of these did not even reach the sixth grade. At the other end of the scale, 8 percent have received at least some university training, a proportion that is well above the Mexican average.[2]

These distributions of occupation, income, and education bear witness both to the substantial impoverishment of the community and to the vast inequalities that exist. In this, Jalapa resembles most urban populations. The range of inequality and differential control of resources needs to be emphasized, nevertheless, not only because it documents societal maldistribution, but also because much of the political life of the city can only be understood against this background. Of particular importance are the overlapping and cumulative characteristics of economic and cultural advantage, and their relationship to the pattern of political activities.[3]

Class and Cumulative Advantage

Patterns of cumulative advantage—and disadvantage—are most easily illuminated by educational data. It can be argued that in an urban setting education begins to bestow special advantages on an individual only when he or she passes beyond primary school, for only in secondary school are the vocational and cultural skills acquired that enable a person to manipulate city-based institutions to his own advantage. From this perspective the man who has but five years of schooling, even though nominally literate, is only marginally better equipped than the first-year dropout or the individual who never went to school at all.

If "more-than-primary" schooling is the criterion, approximately one quarter of the adult population of Jalapa qualifies as educationally advantaged. As might be expected, the incidence of that advantage varies dramatically with both social class and

[2] The 1960 official estimate of literacy in the municipio (79 percent of those over five years of age) is undoubtedly exaggerated. See *VIII Censo General*, Tomo I: Estado de Veracruz, p. 41.

[3] The proposition that rankings of occupation, income, and education are intercorrelated in modern societies is among the most fully documented in the literature dealing with social structure. See Appendix C for a statistical analysis of the relationships between these variables and other socioeconomic (SES) measures in Jalapa.

TABLE 4.3

Distribution by Social Class and Sex of Adults
Having More than Primary Education
(*Percent*)

Class	Men (N = 721)	Women (N = 663)	Combined (N = 1,384)
Upper (N = 165)	85%	55%	73%
Middle (N = 579)	36	18	27
Lower (N = 640)	17	7	12

NOTE: Chi-square = 69.7; *p* < .001.

sex.[4] As indicated in Table 4.3, upper-class men are almost all advantaged, as are slightly more than half the upper-class women. Thereafter, the decline in advantage as one moves down the class structure is precipitous, and within each class women are sharply disadvantaged when compared with men.[5] Few middle-class women and even relatively fewer members of the lower class thus have the educational and cultural background necessary to manage situations requiring relatively modest capabilities in reading, writing, or arithmetic, not to mention situations that demand the more intangible skills associated with post-primary education.

Furthermore, a powerful class bias has operated in the distribution of the increased opportunities for education that have been created over the past decades. As the data in Table 4.4 suggest, the aggregate growth in educational attainment as measured by the schooling of male respondents as opposed to that

[4] Differences between classes and the definitions of the classes themselves as used here must be understood in relation to the general level of development in Mexico and Jalapa. Most of the upper class as here defined have modest average income, educational level, and life-style by North American standards. They are best described not as the rich of Jalapa (although some are), but as the top 10 percent. The class index used here and elsewhere in the book is constructed from the interviewer's assessment of the respondent's socioeconomic status, combined with data on family income. For details on the construction and justification of the index see Appendix C.

[5] In order to avoid artificially inflating the size and thus the statistical significance of the Chi-squares reported in this and the following tables, we based all Chi-square tests on N's (not shown) proportionally reduced to the level of the original (N = 399) sample.

TABLE 4.4

Education of Male Respondents and Their Fathers by Social Class
(Percent)

| | Highest level of education attained | | |
| | Did not finish primary | Finished primary only | Some secondary or more |
Class			
Upper			
Respondents ($N = 98$)	7%	8%	85%
Fathers ($N = 76$)	30	16	54
Middle			
Respondents ($N = 287$)	29	35	36
Fathers ($N = 187$)	43	33	24
Lower			
Respondents ($N = 336$)	65	18	17
Fathers ($N = 212$)	81	15	4
All combined			
Respondents ($N = 721$)	43	23	34
Fathers ($N = 475$)	58	22	20

NOTE: Chi-square (upper class only) $= 12.5$; $p < .01$. Chi-squares for the middle and lower classes were not significant.

of their fathers has accrued disproportionately to the upper class.[6] Stated differently, middle- and lower-class men have risen only marginally above the educational achievements of their fathers, whereas upper-class men have risen significantly—most notably in the critical area of post-primary schooling. Moreover, educational differences between the middle and the lower class in Jalapa are almost as acute today as they were a generation ago, and the gap between each of these two classes and the upper class is now, if anything, greater. In short, members of the upper class, themselves often the children of educationally advantaged fathers, have become even more advantaged while

[6] If data on women (who as a group have less education than men) were included in Table 4.4, the inter-class and inter-generational differences would be even more striking because the educational levels would drop more for both lower- and middle-class respondents than for upper-class respondents. Since only father's education was asked, however, it was decided that the father-son comparison more accurately reflected aggregate educational growth. Given the strong sex bias in the distribution of educational opportunity, we would need data on mother's education in order to assess the full extent of educational mobility and inequality.

members of the other two classes have just about been holding their families' positions in the educational hierarchy.[7] Among our respondents, education is and has been so much a prerogative of the upper class that with little exaggeration it can be said to be as characteristic of their way of life as the houses they live in and the clothes they wear. Moreover, the distinction of higher education is repeatedly reflected in social intercourse. Except among close friends of similar status, it is customary and almost mandatory to address highly educated persons by the appropriate title, such as *ingeniero, arquitecto,* or *profesor.*

As suggested earlier, the finding that educational advantage is concentrated in the upper class comes as no real surprise, although the cumulative nature of this advantage stands as a stark commentary on the distribution of benefits under the so-called continuing Revolution. What is more surprising is the disproportionate extent to which the upper class also enjoys certain political advantages in an institutional setting that is ostensibly geared to the representation of middle- and lower-class interests, the common man, or "el pueblo."

The idea of political advantage is not easily translated into operative terms in the Mexican setting, for those who have top-level contacts and influence are relatively few and hard to identify. Even informants interviewed as part of our elite study tended to note that "influence" was not a good way to describe their access to public decision-making. When asked about influence, most preferred instead to say that they, as individuals, were "cooperating" when they sought government action. Thus we

[7] Lacking an independent measure of the class position of fathers, we cannot make a full analysis of the interaction of class and educational mobility. What is clear, however, is that educational advantage gets passed from father to son, and in those few cases in which it does not there are class correlates of the resulting downward educational mobility. For example, all but two of the 41 upper-class males whose fathers had at least some secondary school have as much education as their fathers, or more. In the middle class, of the 45 sons whose fathers had at least some secondary schooling, 15 did not go beyond primary school. In the lower class, only eight fathers had some secondary schooling, and *none* of their sons went that far.

are not concerned with a "power elite" but rather with those Jalapeños who can be thought of as having an edge of some sort on their fellows when it comes to dealing with the political system. Political advantage is therefore conceptualized quite loosely as accruing to those who have organizational access to government or who have "experience" with authorities. Such people have not necessarily "gotten their way" in dealings with government, but, their modesty in public notwithstanding, they can be considered favorably located in the web of contacts and potential contacts that makes getting one's way more probable. This is what might be called a sociometric view of political advantage, depending as it does on the assumption that opportunities for contact and experiences with authorities are of advantage to the citizen in diffuse but important ways. These contacts and experiences are resources in much the same way that post-primary education is a resource, and their distribution in Jalapa is most illuminating.

In Table 4.5, six items relating to political contacts are tabulated by class and sex.[8] What is immediately obvious is that none of the activities involves a majority of any sector. The data suggest a population that infrequently joins a political party or a politically oriented organization, almost never participates in an electoral campaign, sometimes seeks help from an official but is seldom contacted in return, and almost never tries to influence a governmental decision.

The aggregate levels of activity—or non-activity—are of particular interest, for the Mexican regime encourages structured

[8] Of all respondents, 78 percent claimed to have voted in the 1964 presidential election and 64 percent claimed to have voted in the municipal election of the same year. In each election, women and members of the lower class less frequently said they voted than did men and members of the other two classes. Class differences were smaller than sex differences. The validity if not the pattern of these data is very much in question, however, for all other available information suggests that the percentages are much exaggerated. Failure to vote is technically illegal in Mexico (although widespread), and official voting figures were irretrievable from local archives. Knowledgeable and reliable informants suggested that voting turnout in the 1964 municipal election might actually have been as low as 10 percent. We thus decided to eliminate voting data from our discussion of political activity and contacts.

TABLE 4.5

Responses by Social Class and Sex to Selected Political-Contact Items
(Percent)

| Response | Class | | | Sex | | Total[a] |
	Upper (N = 165– 152)	Middle (N = 587– 509)	Lower (N = 640– 532)	Men (N = 777– 675)	Women (N = 779– 652)	(N = 1,556– 1,327)
(1) Have gone to an official in Jalapa (any level of government) to seek help or support	29%	21%	20%	30%	10%	20%
(2) Do belong to an organization that takes part in or discusses political or public issues or tries to influence government actions	21	11	14	24	2	14
(3) Am a member of a political party (99% of party members are in the PRI)	29	15	6	18	5	11
(4) Have been contacted by a government functionary seeking approval or cooperation in any matter	27	9	3	11	4	8
(5) Have tried to influence a decision related to governmental affairs in Jalapa	10	3	4	6	2	4
(6) Have participated actively in a political campaign (giving speeches, declaring public approval for a candidate, etc.)	8	4	1	5	1	3

[a] Total percentages are not always exactly the weighted average of the class percentages because of missing data on the class index and the consequent reduction in N's. Here and elsewhere in the tables, double figures in parentheses are the high and low N's on which column percentages are based.

and controlled political contacts to a greater degree than per-haps any other in Latin America with the exception of Cuba. In some instances the relatively modest levels of activity found in Jalapa need to be emphasized primarily because the govern-ment makes such outlandish national claims. Official government statistics, for example, can lead one to estimate the total PRI membership as 6.62 million, or better than one out of every three adult Mexicans in the late 1950's.[9] In Jalapa, however, only one out of every nine adults claims Party membership. Although the Jalapan ratio is not necessarily representative of the nation as a whole, it is undoubtedly closer to the real national ratio than are the official figures.

In other instances the Jalapan data are of interest because certain political processes that we have said are important in understanding local governance do not touch so many citizens as one might expect. Just as the data offer a needed corrective to official enthusiasms, so they caution us against imagining that bargaining with public officials is part of the everyday life of very many citizens. With only 8 percent reporting that a gov-ernment functionary has contacted them, and only 4 percent saying that they have tried to influence local affairs, it is clear that the kinds of tax and street-improvement issues described in the previous chapter do not occur often enough to touch the majority of citizens.[10] Jalapeños in general lead a politically

[9] Robert E. Scott, *Mexican Government in Transition,* revised edition, (University of Illinois Press, 1964), p. 167. Another indication of inflated estimates of opportunities for political contact is the widespread notion that most skilled workers in Mexico are unionized (*ibid.,* pp. 73–75). In Jalapa, 63 percent of our skilled-worker respondents said that they did not belong to *any* organizations (labor, religious, civic, etc.) despite being asked spe-cifically about unions. In truth, only certain sectors of the skilled labor force are unionized in Mexico.

[10] There may be a tendency for respondents to understate their contacts through forgetfulness or unwillingness to be associated with activities that they see as somewhat corrupt or dirty. With this in mind, every effort was made to encourage "contact" responses through the phrasing of questions and response categories and through directing the respondent's attention to local and small-scale arenas of action. Furthermore, in Table 4.5 all posi-tive responses were lumped together, giving each item the maximum pos-sible percentage figures. For example, even if a respondent only recalled going to a government official for help once in his life, he was considered active under item 1.

quiet life. There are few open, regularized channels through which the people are encouraged to articulate their grievances, and functionaries make no serious attempts to reach out to the common man except on those relatively rare occasions when administrative obedience is not automatically forthcoming and politicians and bureaucrats begin to worry that civic tranquillity, and thus their image as capable managers, is threatened.

The overall paucity of political contacts is not, however, the only or even the most important message of Table 4.5. It is also clear that some citizens are considerably more active than others. In every instance members of the upper class have more contacts than members of the other two classes, and men have more contacts than women. In fact—although the relevant data are not included in the table—within each class, women are always less active than men, no matter what item is considered. Lower-class women, who comprise one-quarter of the adult population of Jalapa, have virtually no political contacts at all. For most women, and for those of the lower class in particular, woman's place is clearly in the home, shop, or office—certainly not in the political arena, or even in many of the popular cafés, unless escorted by a man. The other side of this imbalance is seen in the statistics for upper-class men. Although they comprise only about 6 percent of the total sample, they account for almost a third of all those who have been contacted by government officials seeking help, and disproportionate percentages of those reporting other organizational affiliations or political contacts.

On certain items, such as attempts to influence governmental affairs, the disproportionate activity of the upper class is not surprising. With most at stake and most resources, it is to be expected that the upper class (men in particular) would most frequently try to affect governmental decisions. But figures such as those on Party membership are less predictable, for they are not consistent with the notion of the popularization of the PRI. Almost one-half of all upper-class men report Party membership; slightly less than a quarter of the middle-class men say they belong; and only 7 percent of the lower-class men are members. In no class does the representation of women exceed

"They're all my children."

7 percent. Looked at differently, of the total PRI membership in Jalapa, 28 percent belong to the upper class (which constitutes about 12 percent of the total population), 51 percent to the middle class (about 42 percent of the total population), and 21 percent to the lower class (46 percent of the total population).

If this is a party in which, as some of its admirers claim, conflicting interests are represented and reconciled, then it is clear whose interests receive disproportionate representation in Jalapa. Although it should not be taken as fully typical of the national situation, the local scenario is undoubtedly repeated with only minor variations in many cities across the Republic. It is a situation in which the male upper class accounts for a sharply disproportionate share of all political contacts and activities and receives, one would assume, a similarly disproportionate share of the resultant gratifications and benefits.

This distribution of contacts—and thus of political advantage as here defined—has the same pattern as the distribution of educational advantage, with men and the upper class disproportionately favored. Although the patterns are similar, it does not however logically follow that those individuals who are educationally advantaged in a given sector are necessarily also those who have political contacts. The model of cumulative advantage *does* imply such a relationship—that class position is related to educational achievements and that both in turn are related to political advantage—but the relationships at the individual level are only suggested, not demonstrated or explored by the data presented above.

In order to examine the relationship between class, education, and political advantage, an index of the latter is needed. In constructing such an index, we gave one point for every activity listed in Table 4.5 in which an individual had been engaged.[11] Thus every respondent received a score of from zero to six. As might be expected, a majority of citizens, almost two out of three, scored zero—they had no political contacts at all. Another 19 percent received only one point, almost 8 percent received two points, and 9 percent received three or more. In the analysis that follows we have considered only those who received two or more points on the index (17 percent) as belonging to the advantaged group. Our advantaged group is hardly more impressive in its linkages to government than it is in size. Its members are simply those who seem a bit better located politically than other citizens; in this sense it is analogous to the educationally advantaged group.

As the data presented in Table 4.5 have suggested, there is a relatively strong relationship between social class and political advantage. This can also be seen in Table 4.6 where the distribution of politically advantaged Jalapeños is shown by social class and education. When all educational levels are combined, 36 percent of upper-class citizens are classified as politically advantaged, whereas the number drops to 20 percent of the middle class and then to 13 percent of the lower class. But of more interest is the interaction of class and education as both relate to

[11] One slight adjustment was made in constructing this index. Six percent of the respondents said that although they were not currently members of a political party, they had been so in the past. These respondents were added to those who said that they currently belonged, thus forming a substitute category (for item 3) of "party members, past and present." It was assumed that in the construction of an index of political advantage, past party membership should also count, just as past visits to government officials contributed to an individual's score.

TABLE 4.6

Distribution of Politically Advantaged Adults by Social Class and Education

(*Percent*)

Class	Did not finish primary ($N = 729$)	Finished primary only ($N = 303$)	Some secondary or more ($N = 352$)	All levels combined ($N = 1,384$)
Upper ($N = 165$)	17%	23%	42%	36%
Middle ($N = 579$)	19	10	35	20
Lower ($N = 640$)	15	9	0	13

NOTE: Chi-square $= 78.6$; $p < .001$.

political advantage. Put bluntly, the message of the table is that the amount of education one has makes if anything a negative difference with respect to political advantage until one crosses the sixth-grade threshold. Then, in the upper and middle classes, increased education is definitely associated with increased political advantage, whereas in the lower class those who have at least some secondary education are uniformly found among the politically *disadvantaged*!

What interpretation can be given to these findings? The case of the middle and upper classes fits well with the model of cumulative advantage and the meaning previously attached to post-primary education. That is, citizens who receive post-primary education—the probabilities of which are deeply conditioned by the class structure—are subsequently more likely than others to locate themselves advantageously with respect to politics. They more frequently seek out and are sought out by those whose business is managing the political system, even in environments that have ostensibly been set up to give the less privileged a break. The structure of political opportunities has been shaped by self-reinforcing perceptions of who counts and who does not. The web of contacts and cooperation on which the political business of the community depends thus more frequently enmeshes citizens of some class standing and education.

The attrition of contacts and advantage among the lower class

as education increases is also consistent with this model of cumulative advantage, albeit for quite different reasons. The key factor in this case is the sharply restricted range of politically relevant opportunities that for structural and historical reasons are
open to members of the underclass, irrespective of their educational attainments. As shown in Table 4.5, the two activities that
account for most lower-class political contacts are membership
in a politically relevant organization and going to an official in
search of support. In most instances among the lower class, these
categories translate into union membership (sometimes accompanied by Party membership) and occasional hat-in-hand visits
to the authorities. The "politically advantaged" lower-class Jalapeño is thus typically a unionized worker, clerk, or marginal
merchant who also either belongs to the Party or has occasionally sought benefits from officials—or both. In some lower-class
occupations that contribute to the ranks of the politically advantaged, the educational level is very low, thus making a relationship between the two kinds of advantage impossible. For example, not one of the 80 lower-class "small businessmen" has
even finished the primary grades, much less attempted secondary school. In other occupations, however, there are more substantial educational attainments. More than half of the 28 lower-
class clerks and almost one-fifth of the 220 skilled and unskilled
workers have at least some secondary schooling; yet not one
member of this atypically well-educated group of working men
(and a few women) is sufficiently participant to be classified as
politically advantaged!

Why should this be the case? Why do educationally advantaged lower-class workers seem to shun the traditional arenas
of lower-class political activity? We do not have the data necessary to examine this question. We can only speculate that as
men who obviously live below what one might expect from their
educational attainments, they feel impelled to withdraw from
public activities and possible embarrassment. Whatever their
reasons, it is clear that the collective political plight of the lower
class can only be made more acute by the nonparticipation of

its most educationally advantaged members. Additionally, it is also clear that across the range of classes, educational advantage does not begin to reinforce political advantage until some minimal level of institutional and psychological opportunities exists; and the lower class in Jalapa, despite the mythology of the Revolution, lives below this minimum.

Acceptance of the Status Quo

The cumulative advantages that accrue to members of the upper and to a lesser extent the middle class are the hallmarks of a system in which advances in the distribution of goods and opportunities have not kept pace with advances in their production. Few if any observers of modern Mexico would dispute that the nation's aggregate economic growth has been impressive over the last decades.[12] What elicits more heated debate is the manner in which economic, social, and political benefits and opportunities have been distributed among various sectors of the population.

For understanding Mexican politics, however, it is not sufficient simply to illuminate the cumulative advantages enjoyed by those who are well placed in the social structure. It is also necessary to appreciate the views that citizens have of the present and future of the socioeconomic system in which they live. Are inequalities perceived? If so, is the response envy, anger, resignation? Are existing social and economic relationships glorified, tolerated, damned? By whom, and with what implications for politics? Such are the kinds of questions to which we now turn.

Table 4.7 presents data from seven questions dealing with social and economic progress, personal satisfactions, and expec-

[12] The most exhaustive treatment of growth and change in the Mexican economy is Clark W. Reynolds, *The Mexican Economy: Twentieth-Century Structure and Growth* (Yale University Press, 1970). Reynolds is quite sensitive to the political and historical sources of growth, but he pays less attention (in part because data are lacking and in part because they are not his primary concerns) to the distributional and sociopolitical consequences of growth.

TABLE 4.7

Responses by Social Class to Items About National Progress and Personal Satisfaction

(Percent)

Questionnaire item and response	Upper class (N = 165–151)	Middle class (N = 587–497)	Lower class (N = 640–548)
(1) How much *economic progress* do you think Mexico—that is, the entire nation—is making?			
A great deal	62%	58%	57%
A little	32	33	33
TOTAL	94%	91%	90%
(2) Personally, how much are you benefiting from this progress?			
A great deal	37%	12%	4%
A little	46	44	31
TOTAL	83%	56%	35%
(3) How much *social progress*—that is, in education, workers' rights, etc.—do you think Mexico is making?			
A great deal	53%	63%	41%
A little	44	31	39
TOTAL	97%	94%	80%
(4) Personally, how much are you benefiting from this progress?			
A great deal	27%	18%	8%
A little	40	47	29
TOTAL	67%	65%	37%
(5) In general, are you satisfied with the way you live today?			
Satisfied to some degree	97%	87%	65%
(6) Thinking of your economic situation in general—that is, the money that you or your family earns—are you satisfied or not?			
Satisfied to some degree	65%	63%	43%
(7) How do you think your economic situation will change in the next ten years?			
Get better	69%	70%	61%
Remain the same	20	17	23
TOTAL	89%	87%	84%

NOTE: See also Table 5.1 for data on satisfaction with influence in community affairs.

tations for the future. These data show, first, that generalized belief in both the economic and social progress of Mexico is strong in all classes. There is widespread public appreciation of the impressive aggregate growth of goods and services. Second, the extent to which citizens see themselves as sharing in that progress is directly related to their class position. Only about a third of the lower class see themselves as sharing in Mexico's progress, whereas in the middle and upper classes the proportions are much greater. A certain relative accuracy of perception is suggested by these responses, although it might seem surprising that even as many as a third of the lower-class respondents could see themselves as sharing in the nation's progress. (Whether or not they really have shared in that progress is a question we cannot answer with our data, and one, moreover, that is probably no more telling than whether they feel as if they have.) In any event, other responses place these in perspective. When asked about satisfaction in general, the upper class is unanimously satisfied, the middle class nearly so, and the lower class substantially so. On economic satisfaction, the proportion of those satisfied in each class drops; in Jalapa as elsewhere economic expectations expand to absorb the available income, creating dissatisfaction at all levels and narrowing the gap in perceptions but not the gap in income between rich and poor. But it is the response pattern to the final item that is most illuminating: in all classes large majorities feel that their economic situation will improve over the next decade. What is particularly striking is the extent to which lower-class citizens, correctly perceiving that they have not shared fully in Mexico's social and economic progress and often dissatisfied with their economic situation, nevertheless expect that their financial condition will improve.

Without doing violence either to common sense or to the diversity of Jalapa, it can be said that the data in Table 4.7 suggest a citizenry that is not deeply distressed over what God, history, and the Mexican economy have wrought. The modal pattern is one of near unanimity on Mexico's progress, less agreement on the extent to which one has shared in that progress, substantial satisfaction with one's life in general, less satisfaction with one's economic condition, and relatively high hopes for the future. The lower class exhibits the sharpest discontinuities in its evaluations, satisfactions, and expectations, but all in all the picture connotes satisfaction, hope, or resignation rather than disappointment or discontent. This mixture of perceptions and evaluations seems to lead citizens toward acceptance of the status quo rather than toward tilting against the socioeconomic order with all that the latter implies in uncertainty and risks.

Our understanding of citizen perceptions of the existing order is deepened by considering responses to a question about differences between rich and poor. When asked if existing differences were too large, too small, or just about right, one-quarter of all respondents answered that they were just about right and another one-fifth said that they ought to be larger![13] The breakdown of responses by class and sex is presented in Table 4.8.

Although class differences are not dramatic in Table 4.8, the distribution of responses is somewhat surprising. From conventional perspectives on the upper and middle classes it might be expected that sizeable minorities would see existing differences as about right or even as less than they should be. Members of the middle class in particular often have at best a tenuous hold on the occupations and possessions that define them as "better" than the underclass. Attracted to a style of life that is often beyond their means, they are also at times only recently escaped

[13] The full question was: "Do you think that the difference between people of high economic position—that is, the rich—and people of low economic position—that is, the poor—is much greater than it ought to be, greater than it ought to be, pretty much as it ought to be, or less than it ought to be?" Note that the structure of the question probably encouraged responses saying that existing differences were too large. Thus, the relatively high percentage of respondents satisfied with existing arrangements or feeling that differences were not great enough is not a consequence of response set. Notice, however, that the question is (unfortunately) ambiguous with respect to the kinds of differences that are under consideration. The majority of respondents undoubtedly understood the question primarily in economic terms, but others were probably thinking in terms of social or cultural differentiation.

TABLE 4.8

Opinion by Social Class and Sex on Differences Between Rich and Poor
(*Percent*)

Response	Class			Sex	
	Upper ($N = 155$)	Middle ($N = 551$)	Lower ($N = 576$)	Men ($N = 697$)	Women ($N = 585$)
Difference is greater than it should be	58%	49%	63%	63%	49%
Difference is about right	28	28	19	18	32
Difference is less than it should be	14	22	17	19	19
TOTAL	100%	99%	99%	100%	100%

NOTE: Some figures total less than 100 percent because of rounding. Chi-square (sex) $= 9.9$; $p < .01$. The Chi-square test for class was not significant.

from poverty and lower-class environments. When persons so located in the status and consumption hierarchy say that differences between rich and poor are not great enough, they may be saying that they wish their incomes were sufficient to remove the ambiguity and fragility that now attaches to their life-style. This interpretation is strengthened by the finding that relative to the middle class, fewer upper-class respondents see differences as less than they should be and more see them as greater than they should be. Members of the upper class are generally secure enough to view the situation with a bit more equanimity. They are less likely to see a blurring of class differences as threatening to their position and prerogatives and thus may be more likely to temper their perspectives with a dash of *noblesse oblige.*

Speculation about the sources of middle- and upper-class perspectives, however, only serves to highlight the seeming anomaly of a lower-class perspective so similar to them in its views of the existing economic order. Setting aside a limited number of respondents who were undoubtedly confused by the content of the question and thus answered "incorrectly," the data indicate that a significant number of Mexicans who are indeed very badly off do accept their station in life or even view a more sharply stratified social order as somehow attractive. How can anyone who lives as do most of the poor in Jalapa feel that there ought to be greater differences between rich and poor or—for that matter—that existing differences are about right? A partial answer is that the uncertainty and threat felt by some members of the middle class seems to exist even at the lower reaches of the economic order. Thus, those "richer" members of the lower class with family incomes between $40 and $80 a month are almost twice as likely as those with incomes below $40 to see differences as less than they should be. There is also a pecking order within the lower class. The psychology of threat and uncertainty is no respecter of our rather arbitrarily drawn class distinctions.

But there may also be another mechanism in operation. Some lower-class Jalapeños may wish for greater economic differentiation precisely because they feel that such an order would be more Christian and responsible, leading to an increase in employment, charity, or public welfare for the underclass. Living with the anxieties and insecurities engendered in an individualistic environment that encourages competition and touts mobility, some members of the lower class (and for that matter some members of the middle class as well), must surely long for the security that comes from being embedded in a definitely stratified corporatist order. This does not imply that such sharply disadvantaged individuals are wishing upon themselves greater hardship or a lesser economic share. Quite to the contrary, theirs is a perfectly rational desire to escape from the freedom of the marketplace into the greater security and personalism of a society that would at least show some collective concern for its underclass, perhaps through the agency of a benevolent patron.

One final group of questions aids in defining Jalapan perspectives on the status quo. Thus far we have documented a conservative thrust in orientations to the existing order and one's present and future place in it. It might thus be expected that proposed changes in the socioeconomic order would be rejected or at least viewed with suspicion by large segments of the population. Is this actually the case? What happens when citizens are asked to "vote" on a number of public policy issues that imply changes in socioeconomic arrangements?[14] Who embraces and who rejects change-oriented policies? The responses reported in Table 4.9 might at first glance suggest, surprisingly, that Jalapeños are by no means so firmly attached to the status quo as has been suggested. Let us examine each item more closely, however. Item 1 restates in question form what many politicians of all persuasions have been telling Mexicans for decades. Stated so generally, it allows respondents to infuse it with whatever content they find most congenial, whether conservative, centrist, or leftist. For businessmen, "basic economic and social changes" might thus mean vigorous encouragement of the private sector; for middle-class housewives it might mean an emphasis on order and morality in the community; for marginally employed members of the underclass it might imply provisions for jobs and food by whatever means. The suggestion that economic and social changes will have to be basic in order for proper development to take place evidently arouses a bit more resistance as one moves up the class hierarchy, but most Jalapeños can accept the idea of the necessity of basic changes as long as they are free to define what those changes ought to be.

Item 2, on land reform, is much the same sort of question. Since the Mexican leadership has for over fifty years celebrated land reform as one of its basic goals, it should not be surprising that over four-fifths of the citizens of Jalapa support it. Nor

[14] In all survey work of this kind there is some risk that responses will reflect an artificially inflated or skewed level of political consciousness. That is, the interviewer may evoke "opinions" from respondents on subjects that they have not previously considered or that fall outside their experience or conceptualization of politics. In Jalapa, however, we feel that this was not a serious methodological problem, for simply by virtue of living in a politically active state capital respondents had been exposed to the topics and problems about which opinion questions were asked. This does not mean, of course, that most respondents were ordinarily interested in or concerned about such topics and problems, but it does suggest that we were not operating outside the realm of indigenous political discourse—an assumption checked at several points in the process of designing and pre-testing the questionnaire.

TABLE 4.9

Supportive Responses by Social Class to Items About Social and Economic Change

(*Percent*)

Questionnaire item and response	Upper class (N = 163–154)	Middle class (N = 567–524)	Lower class (N = 616–572)
(1) Do you think that basic economic and social changes are necessary in Mexico for the country to develop as it should?			
Yes	79%	83%	89%
(2) Would you favor or oppose a land reform program that would divide the large agricultural properties in order to distribute the land among the peasants?			
Favor, but compensate in full	31%	32%	18%
Favor, but compensate in part	45	41	60
Favor, but no compensation	1	11	9
TOTAL	77%	84%	87%
(3) Would you favor or oppose government expropriation—that is, confiscation—of the property of foreigners?[a]			
Favor, but compensate in full	23%	16%	6%
Favor, but compensate in part	35	39	43
Favor, but no compensation	11	18	24
TOTAL	69%	73%	73%
(4) The government should own all industry and control the entire economic life of the country.			
Agree in some form	38%	52%	80%

NOTE: These four items do not form an acceptable Guttman scale. Thus it would seem that we are dealing not with a single ideological dimension but with a loosely interrelated set of perspectives on social and economic change.

[a] Although both *expropriation* and *confiscation* have strong connotations of noncompensation, and "expropriation with full compensation" is technically a contradiction, pre-testing indicated that the question was best understood when asked in this way.

should it be surprising that the lower class supports it somewhat more strongly than the upper class. When responses are coded according to the sub-issue of compensation, however, certain differences become more evident: the lower class more definitely than the other two backs away from compensating owners in full, and at the other extreme the upper class almost completely rejects the notion of no compensation. But in each class, compensation in part is the most frequently embraced alternative, and in the light of past land-reform practices in Mexico this can be considered a vote for what is already being done.

The tendency for the lower class to reject the notion of full compensation is more dramatic in item 3, when the expropriation of foreign property is at issue, than it is in item 2. The idea of paying no compensation at all in such expropriations is again least attractive to the upper class. However, as was the case with land reform, in each class the most frequently mentioned solution to the compensation issue is payment in part—hardly an extreme position, given Mexico's history and the profound nationalistic and xenophobic feelings that can be tapped in discussions of foreign property. As with the first two questions, the response pattern to item 3 may thus be interpreted as reflecting substantial approval of ideas that already are integrated into the rhetoric and sometimes into the policies of quite conventional public officials, even though all three questions are couched in the language of change.

Such is not the case, however, with item 4. Here the economic action proposed is not within the conventional wisdom or rhetoric of Mexican politics. Nevertheless, when presented with the statement that the government should own all industry and control the entire economic life of the country, four out of five members of the lower class, one out of two members of the middle class, and almost two out of five members of the upper class agree in one way or another.[15] This is an impressive aggregate expression of sympathy for state economic control. At the same time, the class differences in concern for property relationships—foreshadowed in responses to items 2 and 3—are much intensified. Economic control is a subject on which lower-class attachment to the status quo is tenuous indeed. At this point in the spectrum of public policy alternatives, even the elastic Revo-

[15] In this context it is worth re-emphasizing that the sector designated as upper class includes many who do not come from families of old wealth. Professionals and high civil servants are in general less conservative than the traditionally wealthy on matters such as public ownership.

lutionary consensus cannot stretch far enough to encompass all Mexicans.

With these elaborations in mind, what overall meaning can be given to the responses in Table 4.9? In the first place, there certainly exists a strong general acceptance of the propriety of substantial governmental intervention in the economy. As noted in the previous chapter, almost all Jalapeños conceive of the city's chief problems in economic terms—broadly defined—and almost all of them also see government as responsible for finding solutions. Strong consensus exists on the intervention issue because it is usually raised in the context of problems that do not seem to be yielding to the normal operation of the system. If there are widespread economic problems, government ought to do something about them. If citizens are too poor to afford basic health, education, and welfare services, government ought to provide them. The primary purpose of governmental action in such cases is to get the system functioning more perfectly for the benefit of all. Both those who are high and those who are low on the social hierarchy can agree on the necessity of taking corrective action.

When the issue has more profound ideological content, however, when change in the system of ownership and enterprise is being suggested, then significant class differences appear. The focus on welfare, services, employment, and reforms designed to implement existing programs is replaced by a focus on property and control. Under the new terms of debate, middle- and upper-class interests are threatened, whereas most members of the lower class, having little real stake in existing patterns of ownership, seem quite willing to see the government own all industry and control the entire economy. For decades—sometimes with high expectations and sometimes with despair—they have looked to government to better their lives. They find nothing upsetting or disturbing about the prospect of the socialization of the economy, especially when their attention is focused on large-scale enterprise. Certainly their property would not be affected. In the middle and upper sectors, however, government ownership and control seem much more of a threat, not only to property but to existing values and lifestyles.[16] Little of the sympathy expressed in the middle and upper sectors for reformist governmental intervention and welfare activities carries over into enthusiasm for basic structural changes.

The patterns of inequality, advantage, opinions, expectations, and satisfactions reviewed here suggest an ordered and hierarchical city whose citizens in general live rather easily with social, economic, and political stratification. This does not mean, however, that they are without critical perspectives on their political system. On the contrary, when given the opportunity to talk about government, to evaluate the men and institutions under which they live, and to relate their own expectations to the performance of the system, they find much to criticize, explicitly or implicitly. But apathy and withdrawal also abound, thus softening and refocusing the political perspectives of Jalapeños. It is to this important amalgam of orientations toward politics that we now turn.

[16] In both the middle and the upper class, women are more likely than men to support government ownership and economic control. It would seem that, like members of the lower class, many women do not see their fortunes as ineluctably bound up with existing patterns of ownership. This is one of the very few times in the entire study when women are found in greater proportion than men on what might be called the anti–status-quo side of an issue.

Five

The Political Orientations of Jalapeños

Some of the harshest words spoken in Jalapa are reserved for the men and institutions vested with public responsibility. Yet if public life is not perceived as the natural terrain of the righteous, neither is it the object of reformist zeal or great personal distress. Most Jalapans have come to terms with politics-as-usual, and their orientations toward government, its officials, and themselves as political actors reflect a rather consistent and stable accommodation to the existing system. It is this web of citizen orientations toward politics that will now be examined.[1]

Images of the City and of Politics

The consensus among Jalapans is that their city—despite its shortcomings—is a good place to live. Attractively located, enjoying an excellent climate, and tranquil, it is the kind of medium-sized city with which a person can feel a real identification. It is big enough to be interesting, yet small enough to be comprehensible and personal. It is also a city in which it is pos-

[1] Political orientations are relatively stable perceptions, beliefs, and evaluations of the political system and the role of the self in the system. Orientations are thus indexed by attitudinal dispositions toward and expectations about self, activity, policies, and institutions. The concept of political culture, infrequently used here and in the following chapter, is more inclusive, encompassing key symbols and patterns of action as well as orientations. For a defense of this inclusivist conceptualization of political culture see Richard R. Fagen, *The Transformation of Political Culture in Cuba* (Stanford University Press, 1969), Chapter 1.

sible to overlook or forgive the inadequacies and suspect behavior of public officials, for expectations are not so high nor frustrations so great as to preclude an accommodation to the imperfect local world.

Thus in general the citizens of Jalapa say that they like their city and feel free to express themselves on local affairs. They also give local government relatively high marks for doing its best to solve the municipio's problems, and more than half of all respondents profess themselves satisfied with the community influence that they possess. Although these responses do not constitute unqualified approval of the municipio, the evidence of satisfaction is considerable. Furthermore, as Table 5.1 shows, with the exception of a slight lessening of satisfaction with community influence among the lower class, class differences in these responses are insignificant. A rough consensus on the virtues of Jalapa thus characterizes its citizens. Even the otherwise much-maligned government is seen by almost three out of four adults as doing its best to solve the most serious problems of the city.[2] Although expressed satisfaction with the performance of the government often amounts to forgiving it for its inadequacies rather than praising it for its initiatives, Jalapeños are clearly not up in arms about what government is doing or failing to do.

When attention is focused on specific aspects of the local political scene, however, neither men nor institutions fare so well. Respondents were asked three questions specifically about politics in Jalapa: one about the behavior of public officials, one about the importance of municipal elections, and one about how local decisions are made. As can be seen in Table 5.2, a majority of the citizens perceive public officials in Jalapa as self-serving,

[2] The wording "government here in Jalapa" as used in the question is somewhat ambiguous and was probably understood by most respondents to refer to state and national levels as well as the ayuntamiento. Thus, it is not possible to isolate citizen perceptions of the ayuntamiento as an institution. It is our impression, however, that the ayuntamiento is the object of more derision and criticism than either state or national government. Citizens are often also very much aware of the handicaps under which government labors when it attempts to improve local conditions.

TABLE 5.1

Attitudes Toward Jalapa (Selected Items) by Social Class
(*Percent*)

Questionnaire item and response	Upper class (*N* = 165–163)	Middle class (*N* = 583–545)	Lower class (*N* = 628–584)	Combined (*N* = 1,532–1,440)[a]
(1) Although Jalapa may not be perfect, I think it offers just about everything a person could want.				
Agree in some form	76%	78%	72%	76%
(2) Any citizen of Jalapa who wishes to express himself on important local matters is free to do so.				
Agree in some form	88	83	83	84
(3) Do you think that the government here in Jalapa does everything possible to solve the most urgent or serious problems affecting the city?				
Yes	71	77	69	73
(4) Would you like to have more influence in community affairs than you now have, or are you satisfied with the influence that you now have?				
Satisfied	66	59	50	56

[a] Combined percentages are not always exactly the weighted average of the class percentages because of missing data on the class index and the consequent reduction of *N*'s. Both within classes and in the combined figures, differences between men and women are not great. Where differences do occur, women are usually better satisfied than men.

and there is near consensus on the uselessness of voting in local elections and the elitism of the decision-making process.

Any interpretation of the data in Table 5.2 must recognize from the start that from most perspectives it certainly *is* useless to vote in municipal elections in Jalapa (item 2) and local decisions normally *are* made by a very small group (item 3). If citizens had denied these assertions in any greater proportion than they did, their incapacity to understand local realities would need to be explained. As it is, some citizens might defend elec-

TABLE 5.2

Responses by Social Class to Items About Politics in Jalapa
(*Percent*)

Questionnaire item and response	Upper class (N = 159–139)	Middle class (N = 547–494)	Lower class (N = 608–532)	Combined (N = 1,436–1,327)[a]
(1) Do you think that the majority of public officials in Jalapa are trying to help the community in general, or are they trying to advance their personal interests? Advancing personal interests	44%	63%	66%	62%
(2) It is useless to vote in municipal elections because our leaders are pre-selected by the Party. Agree in some form	76	77	89	82
(3) Almost all the decisions in Jalapa are made by a very small group of local people. Agree in some form	86	79	90	85

[a] Combined percentages are not always exactly the weighted average of the class percentages because of missing data on the class index and the consequent reduction of N's. Within classes, in most instances, differences between men and women are not great. Where differences do occur (in the middle class in particular and to a lesser extent in the upper class), women are more likely to view the local system as closed and elitist.

tions as useful for the display of solidarity they afford, but even the heartiest patriots seldom dare defend them as the means whereby leaders are chosen. As one informant, a high state official and PRI member, said, "Our Party is the majority party. Even more, we don't have any opponents in Jalapa. We totally control elections here, and everyone supports the Party. It is the Party that elects the mayor by an internal selection process." But item 1 is of a slightly different order. Here there is not so clearly a "correct" or "incorrect" response, for the motivations of public officials are mixed and the respondents' experiences condition their perceptions of politicians and bureaucrats. Thus honest men may differ on the extent to which officials are trying to help the community, and these differing perspectives are reflected in the lesser amount of agreement on this item. Nevertheless, almost two out of three Jalapeños select the negative option, and this predominant distrust of the motives of public men profoundly affects relations between government and citizens, particularly when people are being asked to cooperate in or contribute financially to official projects.

It should be noted that although differences between classes on the three items of Table 5.2 are not great, skepticism tends to be more prevalent among the lower classes. In all classes, those with less education tend to be more skeptical. At least in perceptions of local affairs, the lower class and the poorly educated of Jalapa seem to have an edge on others in regard to accuracy and lack of illusions. It is also true, of course, that the well educated and the upper class tend to get better service from local public officials; thus, it is to be expected that they would perceive officials as serving the community more often than would those who are themselves poorly served. The basic point stands: education increases satisfaction and acceptance of the mythology that supports local political practices.

The cynicism and negativism noted in the attitudes of Jalapeños toward local political affairs are if anything more pronounced when citizens view politics in general. This can be seen in the items reported in Table 5.3, all relatively abstract statements about politicians and the political process without reference to specific persons or places.[3] All are opinion items in the spirit of item 1 in Table 5.2: there are no clearly correct or incorrect answers. Furthermore, respondents in general tend to give affirmative answers, to agree with the interviewer on such items. Thus, in the first four items, where disapproval is registered by an affirmative response, the percentages of negativism

[3] The only direct basis for comparing respondents' attitudes toward politics in Jalapa and politics in general comes from the data on item 1 in Table 5.2 and item 2 in Table 5.3. Although the questions are not exactly comparable, they are quite similar. In the question with a local referent, 62 percent give answers connoting negativism toward the performance of public officials. In the general question, 89 percent give such answers. At the end of Chapter 6, an index of cynicism toward politics in Jalapa is introduced. Scores on that index correlate highly with scores on the general negativism scale developed in this section.

TABLE 5.3

Critical Responses to Selected General Items About Politics
(*Percent*)

Questionnaire item and response	All respondents ($N = 1,503-1,386$)
(1) All the candidates make beautiful speeches, but one never knows what they will do after they come to power. Agree in some form	95%
(2) It is said that certain persons or groups have a lot of influence in running the government, influence that they use to their own advantage while forgetting the well-being of the people. Agree in some form	89
(3) Political activity exposes one to a great deal of unpleasantness and dirt. Agree in some form	74
(4) Every politician is a crook. Agree in some form	64
(5) In general, the government applies the laws fairly. Disagree in some form	28
(6) Our electoral system is just and honest. Disagree in some form	26

are quite high. In the final two items, where in order to express disapproval respondents would have had to disagree with a stated proposition, percentages drop dramatically. Therefore, although the degree of negativism expressed overall is impressive, one should not attach too much importance to the absolute value of any given percentage.

In order to simplify the analysis and to reduce the influence of this response set toward affirmative answers, all six questions were combined into a scale of negativism toward politics.[4] What

[4] This is a seven-point Guttman scale, here trichotomized by combining scores 0 to 2 (low, 29 percent of respondents), 3 and 4 (medium, 54 percent), and 5 and 6 (high, 17 percent). Details of scale construction will be found in Appendix C. A useful discussion of response set, emphasizing its class correlates, is Henry A. Landsberger and Antonio Saavedra, "Response Set in Developing Countries," *Public Opinion Quarterly*, 31.2, (summer

is most striking about this scale is that with few exceptions it fails to differentiate citizens on the most common demographic dimensions. All age and educational groups are distributed similarly on the scale, and class and sex differences are muted except for the disproportionate tendency for men to be highly negative.[5]

What interpretation should be given to such a finding? The least charitable is that the scale is not very meaningful, for it fails to relate to the common demographic variables. More plausible, we think, is the interpretation that negativism is distributed relatively equally throughout the population because all citizens partake of certain aspects of a common political culture. What this implies is that all citizens share to some degree a common learning experience about politics in general, and this experience tends to be predominantly negative no matter what one's age, class, sex, or education. This learning experience need not consist exclusively or even predominantly of actual encounters with public officials and politics. Quite to the contrary, it might best be thought of as the Jalapan counterpart of Victorian orientations toward sex. Even those who are not politically "experienced" in Jalapa seem to have imbibed quite deeply of an *ambiente* in which politics and politicians are seen as self-serving and slightly obscene. For example, although many of the private rewards of political office remain obscure, such things as the new mansion of an ex-governor tend to confirm the

---

1967): 214–29. Note, however, that in Jalapa the product-moment correlation coefficient of the negativism scale and the (seven-point) class index is .04.

[5] The only trace of a consistent demographic relationship is between age and negativism ($r = .11$—negativism increases slightly with age). There is, however, a slight but significant relationship between negativism and two social-psychological variables, "trust in people" ($r = -.17$) and "authoritarianism" ($r = .12$). These two measures have no overt political content, deriving instead from a respondent's perceptions and evaluations of other people, authority relations, and the world in general. Despite the frequent use of such measures in discussions of political orientations and behavior, we have chosen not to pursue this line of analysis further. It is our feeling that the immense complexity of the relationship between social character and the operation of a political system cannot be responsibly explored with our data. For details of the construction of the trust-in-people index and the authoritarianism scale, see Appendix C.

LA SUCESION PRESIDENCIAL NO es NINGUN PROBLEMA: TODOS NUESTROS
POLITICOS son REVOLUCIONARIOS PATRIOTAS HONRADOS Y APASIONADOS
de la JUSTICIA SOCIAL

*"The presidential succession is really no problem: all our políticos are
revolutionaries, patriots, men of honor, and devotees of social justice."*

public's worst suspicions. Jalapeños also cannot help noticing
the late-model automobiles driven by (or for) many state-level
políticos whose formal salaries hardly cover such a luxury—or
benefits like free license plates granted to local favorites such as
especially cooperative journalists.

Furthermore, those who have actually had contact with politics and public officials are the most negative of all. Using the
index of political contact reported in the preceding chapter, we
divided respondents into two groups, those who had no contact
at all (64 percent) and those who had one or more contacts (36
percent). Only one out of eight of the no-contact respondents
scored high on negativism whereas one out of four of the some-
contact respondents scored high. Conversely, the percentage of
the no-contact group scoring low on negativism was significantly
higher than the percentage of the some-contact group. This relationship between contact and negativism is not affected by controls for class and education. It would seem that if a citizen
actually comes into contact with the political process in other
than routine fashion, he or she is more likely to be extremely
negative about politics. This is not a dynamic that leads one to
be optimistic about the part played by participation in forming
positive orientations toward the political process. Not only do

many Jalapeños without real political experience develop negative orientations toward politics, but the minority that is at least marginally active seems to become even more negative as a result of that activity.[6]

Self and Politics

To this point the emphasis has been on what Jalapeños think of their city, its governance, and politics in general. Now we shift our attention to what they think of themselves as political actors in the context of the local system and the climate of negativism just discussed. This focus of attention has been implied in certain prior questions about Jalapa and its problems, but it is here made explicit.

The primary issue is the extent to which the citizen sees himself as having power to affect events and decisions relevant to his life. Following what has now become fairly conventional usage, such perceptions of the self as a political actor will be called a sense of political efficacy.[7] Such a sense should not be confused with the real power a citizen possesses, for as many contemporary authors have pointed out, it is entirely possible for individuals to think that they have some effective control over political outcomes when in fact they are almost completely powerless. But Jalapans, as suggested by the data in Table 5.4, have no such inflated or unrealistic sense of political efficacy. Not many feel that they would or could do much if threatened by an "unjust or prejudicial regulation" and even fewer feel that they can do anything about the local problem they had previously called the most serious in their city.

---

[6] The causal ordering implied, that political activity contributes to one's orientation, is the reverse of that most frequently suggested in research of this sort. To argue that the more negative one is toward politics, the more likely one is to be active seems ludicrous. When Jalapeños participate, it is most likely that they do so in spite of their negativism toward politics.

[7] This usage of political efficacy is the same as the notion of subjective civic competence as used by Gabriel A. Almond and Sidney Verba in *The Civic Culture* (Princeton University Press, 1963), pp. 180–89. In what follows, the short form "political efficacy" will be used synonymously with "a sense of political efficacy."

TABLE 5.4

Incidence of a Sense of Political Efficacy
(*Percent*)

Questionnaire item and response	All respondents
(1) Speaking of the local problems here in Jalapa, how well can you understand them?[a]	
Well or very well	24%
More-or-less well	46
TOTAL	70%
(2) Suppose a law or regulation that you considered very unjust or prejudicial to your interests or to the interests of people like yourself were being considered by the municipal government of Jalapa. Do you think you could do anything about it?	
Yes[b]	22
(3) If such a case actually arose, how probable is it that you would really do something to try to change it? (refers to item 2 above)	
Probable or very probable	13
(4) If you were to make an effort to change this law or regulation, how probable is it that you would be successful? (refers to item 2)	
Probable or very probable	11
(5) Can you yourself do anything to solve the major problem of Jalapa? (the problem mentioned by the respondent; see Chapter 3)	
Say they can do something	9

[a] This is less specifically an efficacy item. It is included because it defines the lowest end of the efficacy concept.
[b] Only item 2 can be compared directly with the Almond-Verba data on subjective civic competence. In *The Civic Culture*, p. 185, 52 percent of the Mexican respondents said that they could do something about an unjust local law as opposed to 22 percent of Jalapeños. However, only 6 percent of the *Civic Culture* respondents said that they had ever *tried* to influence a local decision. The corresponding figure for our sample is 4 percent.

In the previous chapter, it was noted that political contacts are relatively infrequent in Jalapa, ranging from a high of 20 percent of respondents who have gone to an official seeking help to a low of 3 percent who have participated actively in a political campaign. The levels of efficacy reported in Table 5.4 are thus quite similar to the levels of political contact documented earlier. Additionally, it was noted that political contacts are dispro-

TABLE 5.5

Distribution by Social Class and Education of Citizens with a High Sense of Political Efficacy

(*Percent*)

	Scoring high on efficacy scale (N = 302)				
Class	Men (N = 729)	Women (N = 663)	All respondents (N = 1,392)	Education	Scoring high on efficacy scale (N = 302)[a]
Upper	55%	21%	41%	Some secondary or more	38%
Middle	23	14	19	Finished primary only	9
Lower	13	8	11	Did not finish primary	15

NOTE: Chi-square (sex by class) = 32.5; $p < .001$; Chi-square (education) = 24.9; $p < .001$. When social class is controlled for educational level, many but not all of the class-related and some of the sex-related differences disappear. As was argued previously, however, higher education should be thought of as a resource accumulated by the upper class, not as a wholly independent factor.

[a] Percentages in this column are based on $N = 1,547$.

portionately the province of men, members of the upper class, and those with higher education. In a political culture like that of Jalapa, with sharply cumulative patterns of opportunities, resources, and activity, it is to be expected that individuals with a highly developed sense of efficacy will also be found disproportionately in the same social sectors. When a scale of political efficacy is constructed from the items in Table 5.4—plus one additional item—this is in fact found to be the case.[8] Data are presented in Table 5.5.

Implied in the comparison of levels and patterns of distribution of political contact and efficacy is the idea that the two variables are themselves interrelated. Both common sense and social theory suggest that those who have more political contacts should also have a stronger sense of political efficacy. The causal

[8] The additional item is "Some people say that political problems are so complicated and difficult that the average citizen cannot understand them (true, partially true, etc.)." The data yield a quasi-Guttman scale of four points, collapsed from six because three of the questionnaire items are logically interrelated (see Appendix C). High-efficacy individuals (about 20 percent of the weighted sample) are those who fall in the top two positions on the scale.

ordering of this relationship is commonly thought to be circular, with a sense of efficacy leading to increased political activity and increased activity in turn leading to a strengthening of one's sense of efficacy.

In fact, respondents with some contact do come disproportionately from among those with higher efficacy. Fifty percent of the high-efficacy respondents ($N = 302$) report some political contact, whereas only 35 percent of those with medium efficacy ($N = 673$) and 30 percent of those with low efficacy ($N = 581$) report such contacts. But almost all these differences can be accounted for by the higher social class, degree of education, and proportion of men among those with high efficacy and political contacts. In other words, a sense of efficacy cannot really be disentangled from the other strands in the web of advantage and disadvantage previously discussed. Those who feel unable to affect local politics are those who are least well situated and equipped to do so. The converse is also the case. Thus the generally low level of perceived efficacy among Jalapans implies not so much a failure of civic education as an accurate perception of reality.

Another dimension of the relationship of an individual to the political system is what Almond and Verba have called "expectations of treatment by government and police."[9] The basic issue here is the extent to which a citizen expects to receive the same treatment as others and to be listened to when he must deal with the authorities. Responses to the four relevant items from our survey are reported in Table 5.6.

It is apparent that a majority of Jalapeños expect that they

[9] See Almond and Verba, *op. cit.*, pp. 106–14. Although asking essentially the same four questions that we subsequently asked in Jalapa, Almond and Verba failed to distinguish between respondents who expected unequal treatment in the direction of being favored and those who expected unequal treatment in the direction of being discriminated against. They lumped both kinds of responses together as "expect unequal treatment." As the response patterns to items 1 and 3 in Table 5.6 suggest, however, this is a critical distinction to make on both conceptual and empirical grounds. In Jalapa, "expecting to be treated better" is a relatively common (and realistic) response among the socially and educationally advantaged.

TABLE 5.6

Expected Treatment by Government and Police

(*Percent*)

Questionnaire item and response	All respondents (N = 1,384)
(1) Suppose there were some question that you had to take up with one of the government offices here in the city—do you think you would be treated in the same manner as any other person?	
No, better	14%
Yes, the same	48
No, worse	24
It depends	13
TOTAL	99%
(2) If you tried to explain your point of view to the officials of that office, do you think they would pay attention to you?	
Yes, a great deal	19%
Yes, a little	37
No, ignore completely	34
It depends	10
TOTAL	100%
(3) If you had some trouble with the police— for instance, if you were accused of a minor infraction—do you think you would be treated in the same manner as any other person?	
No, better	18%
Yes, the same	39
No, worse	29
It depends	15
TOTAL	101%
(4) If you tried to explain your point of view to the police, do you think they would pay attention to you?	
Yes, a great deal	16%
Yes, a little	43
No, ignore completely	29
It depends	11
TOTAL	99%

NOTE: Some totals differ from 100% because of rounding. In the Almond and Verba data on Mexico, the distributions of responses to what are here called items 2 and 4 are very similar to response patterns in Jalapa. See *The Civic Culture*, p. 109. For reasons mentioned in the text, direct comparisons with *Civic Culture* data are not possible on items 1 and 3.

will be treated at least as well as their fellow citizens and that they will be listened to by the authorities. The response patterns are remarkably similar for all four items, with the proportion of respondents feeling that they would be poorly treated or ignored varying from a fourth to a third.[10] In a city where a majority of citizens feel that public officials are trying to advance their own interests, where negativism toward politics is so prevalent, and where a sense of political efficacy is so uncommon, it may seem surprising that so many expect at least equal treatment and a moderately attentive hearing. Certainly, where cynicism and apathy are the modal patterns, the substantial level of expectations of equal treatment by police and government officials can be considered a counter-trend of positive affect toward the system. Many Jalapeños, including those who do not normally command political resources or engage in political activities, face the civil authorities with some confidence that should the need arise they will fare as well as others.

These feelings reflect not only a widespread adaptation to the personalistic textures of encounters between citizen and bureaucrat, but also a substantial reserve of political self-esteem. Even persons who do not think of themselves as efficacious and who do not attempt to influence public policy, see themselves as the equal of their fellows in face-to-face contacts with representatives of the authorities. This does not mean that they always expect to "win" such encounters, but that they expect to be listened to and not be demeaned in the process. For one thing, all but the most underprivileged and isolated Jalapeños usually approach the authorities through the intervention and with the support of others—a friend, relative, *compadre*, or employer who has better connections. The consequences of this style— slightly exaggerated—were expressed by one exasperated federal bureaucrat who commented, "In this country there is always

10 These items do not form an acceptable Guttman scale, in part because the response patterns are too similar. Thus, instead of a scale, a simple index running from 0 to 4 was constructed by coding the first two response categories to each item as "1" and the second two as "0" and then summing across all four items. This index is used in Table 5.7.

a person who knows somebody who knows someone who knows the president." In any event, such personalized approaches usually guarantee at least a polite and outwardly sympathetic hearing if not a successful outcome. Moreover, the importance attached by the regime to the symbol of the open door—officials at all levels are expected to be seen listening to the people, especially to the common man—guarantees considerable access of at least a superficial sort. To the extent that this tone predominates in small-scale political and administrative transactions in Jalapa —only a medium-sized city—it clearly acts as a partial counterweight to the orientations noted earlier.

There is, however, another side to the data presented in Table 5.6. Let us turn for a moment to those who are the lowest in their expectations of equal treatment and attention, those who do not expect to do very well in encounters with police and government officials. Approximately one-third of all respondents fall into the lowest two categories on the index that combines responses to the four items of Table 5.6. These are the citizens who in general expect to be treated worse than their fellows and to be ignored. Who are these unfortunates? As might be expected, they are disproportionately members of the lower class and those with limited education. Somewhat surprisingly, women are found only slightly more frequently than men among those with the lowest expectations of equal treatment, but in all other instances the now familiar pattern of cumulative disadvantage and self-perceptions holds. Data are presented in Table 5.7.

Thus, even though citizens who expect equal treatment are much more frequently found in Jalapa than citizens with a high sense of political efficacy, the distributive patterns of these two orientations are quite similar. In both instances there exists a "hard core" of about one-third of the population that views itself as consigned to powerlessness and unequal treatment in dealings with representatives of the political system.[11]

[11] The efficacy scale and the equal-treatment index are correlated, but many who score low on one do not score low on the other. Thus, the two "hard core" groups overlap but are not the same.

TABLE 5.7

Distribution by Social Class and Education of Low Expectations
Regarding Treatment by Government and Police
(*Percent*)

Class	Reporting low expectations (N = 507)			Education	Reporting low expectations (N = 1,538)[a]
	Men (N = 729)	Women (N = 663)	All respondents (N = 1,384)		
Upper	4%	16%	9%	Some secondary or more	15%
Middle	25	38	32	Finished primary only	29
Lower	43	40	41	Did not finish primary	42

NOTE: Chi-square (sex by class) = 13.3; $p < .01$; *Chi-square* (education) = 15.8; $p < .001$. If this table had isolated instead the approximately 25 percent of respondents who scored highest on the equal-treatment index, a mirror image of the distribution seen here would have resulted. When social class is controlled for educational level, some of the class-related difference disappears. See, however, the note to Table 5.5.
[a] Percentages in this column are based on $N = 1,538$.

Even cursory familiarity with Mexico attests to the essential accuracy of these self-perceptions. Certainly upper-class status, higher education, and maleness are conducive to "getting one's way" or at least getting an attentive hearing in Jalapa and elsewhere in Mexico; and conversely, those without status and education normally do not fare very well. A common laborer who thinks he will be treated like a distinguished lawyer if picked up by the police is likely to suffer a rude awakening, but few laborers harbor such illusions. Citizens may be unrealistic or given to fantasy when they view the system abstractly or on the national level, but closer to the daily round of life the average Jalapan does not often misinterpret or romanticize his world.

Perspectives on Democratic Practice

When Jalapeños are given the opportunity, they agree overwhelmingly with statements that represent the standard liberal democratic verities. Thus in no social class does agreement with any of the following three statements fall below 90 percent: democracy is the best form of government; public officials should be chosen by majority vote; every citizen should have an equal chance to influence government policy. As has been found wherever these general statements have been put to a public opinion referendum, almost everyone subscribes to them.[12] Jalapans are no exception. But because of their platitudinous formulation and the near unanimity with which they are accepted, the statements are not of much help in our attempt to understand the political orientations of Jalapeños. Like resolutions on freedom and motherhood, they are of no use in differentiating levels and patterns of support.

On the other hand, when more specific questions are asked regarding the constitutional rights of minorities, opposition groups, women, and illiterates to free expression and the franchise, the general celebration of democratic procedural values is not sustained.[13] This, too, is a pattern commonly found. The extent and pattern of the rejection of democratic practices are reported in Table 5.8. Since the data reveal some interesting variations by item and class, we shall present interpretations of responses to specific questions before attempting an overall evaluation.

The first configuration worth noting is that responses to items 1 and 2—which are general rather than specific statements—approach the level of agreement and support found for the democratic platitudes mentioned above. In fact, these two statements are extensions and partial specifications of the original three. Levels of agreement ranging from 80 to 90 percent are thus not surprising. By contrast, items 5–8, which all refer specifically to actions involving freedom of speech and are thus derivative of items 1 and 2, are answered in anti-democratic ways

[12] James W. Prothro and Charles M. Grigg, in "Fundamental Principles of Democracy: Bases of Agreement and Disagreement," *Journal of Politics*, 22. 2 (May 1960): 276–94, were the first to use these items.

[13] Democratic values are here defined in quite conventional if limited fashion as universal suffrage, minority rights, and free expression. We were interested in eliciting responses to a limited number of projected actions that we thought would be meaningful to citizens. Furthermore, we wanted the advantages to be gained when a line of questioning that has been used elsewhere is repeated in a different setting.

TABLE 5.8

Support for Democracy and Democratic Practices by Social Class
(Percent of Supportive Responses)

Questionnaire item and response	Upper class (N = 164–157)	Middle class (N = 575–541)	Lower class (N = 624–588)	Combined (N = 1,288–1,364)
(1) The minority should be free to criticize majority decisions. Agree	91%	81%	87%	85%
(2) The minority should be free to try to influence the opinions of the majority. Agree	88	81	81	82
(3) Should the voting law be changed so that only men have the right to vote? No	82	72	64	70
(4) Should the voting law be changed so that only those who can read and write have the right to vote? No	64	66	72	68
(5) Suppose someone wanted to give a speech in Jalapa against the PRI—should he be allowed to? Yes	71	58	42	52
(6) Do you think the government ought to suppress newspapers and magazines that present an unfavorable picture of life in Mexico? No	60	39	43	44
(7) Do you think a member of the Communist Party of Mexico should be allowed to give a speech in Jalapa?[a] Yes	61	46	35	43
(8) Suppose someone wanted to give a speech in Jalapa against the Catholic Church and religion—should he be allowed to? Yes	59	40	39	42

[a] When asked if they thought that a man could believe in Communism and still be a loyal Mexican, 63 percent of the upper class, 75 percent of the middle class, and 77 percent of the lower class said No.

by a majority or near majority of citizens. Thus, support for the minority's freedom to criticize majority decisions and its freedom to influence the opinions of the majority evaporates in large measure when the minority includes anti-PRIistas, anti-Catholics, Communists, or newspapers that present an unfavorable picture of life in Mexico.

Why should this be the case? In general, anti-democratic responses seem to derive from the attachment to the status quo discussed above. Communists, anti-Catholics, critical newspapers, and even anti-PRIistas are all perceived as disruptive to some degree. A citizen may pay lip service to minority expression, but when this minority assumes flesh and brings "Communist" and "anti-Mexican" messages, it is seen as potentially destructive of the valued quietude of public and private life. Thus, those who are perceived as potential troublemakers in the public arena—and this list is long and inclusive—are in effect told by many citizens that they should go make their mischief elsewhere, leaving Jalapa, imperfect as it might be, with its institutions unchallenged and its public life undisturbed.

Within this general *ambiente* of hostility toward those who might make waves in the community, there is a specific tendency for support of democratic practices to diminish among the middle and especially among the lower class. In part this reflects the frequently documented relationship between tolerance of dissent and higher education. One of the values that higher education has traditionally upheld in Western societies is freedom of speech. Thus it is not surprising to find that if educational level is controlled on items 5–8, most of the observed class differences can be accounted for. As argued previously, however, this is hardly a demonstration of the independent effect of education, for in Jalapa class and education are tightly linked.

A more pointed speculation is that the perceived threat of the kinds of activities suggested in items 5–8 is greater among those who are socially and politically marginal. According to this line of reasoning, *marginales*—often living on the edge of personal catastrophe—are often more conservative in life-style than those who are more securely located in the socioeconomic hierarchy. They are less ready to accept challenges to church, state, or culture—sources of stability and comfort in the environments that they know. Furthermore, their collective experience with agitators, iconoclasts, and dissenters has not been especially happy. Historically, social and political unrest has been quick to dislocate and trouble them but painfully slow to benefit them—if in fact it benefits them at all. The image of speeches being given in Jalapa by Communists, anti-PRIistas and anti-religionists looks very much like the first stirrings of unwanted social and political unrest. Whatever they may feel about the difficulties and hardships under which they labor, they do not see these speechmakers and their doctrines as saviors.[14]

These data, taken in conjunction with those at the end of the previous chapter, reaffirm the oft-noted pattern in which the lower classes are more supportive of reform-oriented economic programs and at the same time less supportive of democratic political practices. A classic early formulation of this pattern was given by Seymour Martin Lipset: "The poorer strata everywhere are more liberal or leftist on economic issues; they favor more welfare state measures, higher wages, graduated income taxes, support of trade-unions, and so forth. But when liberalism is defined in noneconomic terms—as support of civil liberties, internationalism, etc.—the correlation is reversed. The more well-to-do are more liberal, the poorer are more intolerant."[15] Lipset then elaborates a theory of "working-class authoritarianism," that culminates in lower-class participation in "extremist" (which to him usually means Communist) movements. Except for this final link with "extremism," there are some suggestive elements in his chain of theorizing, especially in his description of the con-

---

[14] This interpretation is supported by data on women who—even when education and social class are controlled—still tend to be found more frequently than men among those who would deny freedom of expression to the groups under consideration. In terms of woman's social and political marginality in Jalapa (and Mexico) this is a predictable and consistent outcome.

[15] Seymour Martin Lipset, *Political Man* (Garden City, New York, 1960), pp. 101–2.

ceptual impoverishment brought about by lower-class life and the social and psychological set toward authoritarianism that often grows out of that life-style. But in his zeal to establish the new middle class as the real bearers of the democratic tradition, he and those who subscribe to the theory overlook the simplest explanation of all, one which is certainly applicable in Jalapa: the lower class for rather obvious reasons has least allegiance both to the economic system and to conventional democratic political rhetoric. Neither has served its members particularly well, and it is not inconsistent that although fearing some changes, they also at times articulate positions that imply other changes—especially those of obvious and immediate personal benefit. That this syndrome of low allegiance, fear of change, and frank recognition of self-interest gets characterized as "liberalism" in one instance and "illiberalism" in the other reflects the bias of the observer, not the real world of the poor.

For an additional perspectve on the patterning of anti-democratic orientations, let us return for a moment to items 3 and 4 of Table 5.8, the proposed changes in the voting law. Responses to item 3—the proposed disenfranchisement of women—follow the pattern noted for items 5–8 with the lower class being most ready to take the vote away. In this instance, however, class differences are attributable mainly to variations among the men. Only 13 percent of the upper-class men would deprive women of the vote, whereas 22 percent of the middle-class and 42 percent of the lower-class men would do so. Women, on the other hand, while hardly uniformly protective of their voting rights show less class-related variation. Overall, 30 percent of the women would deprive themselves of the vote, but the range runs only from a low of 24 percent among upper-class women to a high of 34 percent in the middle class with the lower class midway between.[16]

[16] Women voted for the first time in a national election in 1958. Thus, their enfranchisement was less than a decade old when our survey was conducted. Evidently the idea of extending the vote to women did not meet with very rapid or complete approval among the supposed beneficiaries of the change.

Turning now to item 4, in which Jalapeños were asked if the franchise should be limited to those who can read and write, we find a reversal of the dominant response pattern. Here, as in no other item in Table 5.8, the lower class appears as the most supportive of democratic practices. This pattern, of course, indicates some sensitivity to an objective and obvious class interest, for introducing literacy requirements into the voting law would disproportionately disenfranchise members of the lower class. Moreover, the inter-class variation reported is due entirely to differences among the men. While changing the law to limit voting to literates is advocated by slightly fewer women than men (28 percent as opposed to 34 percent), among the women there are no significant class-related differences at all. Among men, however, 42 percent of the upper class, 41 percent of the middle class, and only 27 percent of the lower class support the change. In general, those citizens who are themselves most politically active and advantaged are also most responsive to the suggestion that those who are least advantaged should be excluded from the vote.

A possible interpretation of this particular concentration of anti-democratic sentiment among upper- and middle-class men is suggested by data from the student survey.[17] Among university students, 50 percent of those who are most active politically would deny the vote to illiterates. The proportion of politically active students expressing this sentiment is higher than the proportion among the less active students or any other group or stratum in Jalapa. At the same time, these active students give a far higher proportion of democratic responses on all freedom-of-expression items than does any stratum of the general population. Thus, they exaggerate trends found among the citizenry at large. The franchise for illiterates seems to be perceived by many students not as a democratic right but rather as a device by which politicians assure their continuance in power through demagoguery and the manipulation of the innocents. (There is substantiation for this view in the overwhelmingly high percen-

[17] See Tuohy and Ames, pp. 12–14.

tages of the vote that the PRI normally receives in rural and less developed areas; electoral competition—where it exists—is found in urban, more developed areas.) They thus embrace the elitist position of the limited franchise as the lesser of two evils, an alternative that might introduce a competitive corrective into the system. With our data, there is no way to tell whether other citizens share this analysis of the situation or whether upper- and middle-class males simply view illiterates as a potentially dangerous rabble, and feel threatened by the knowledge that they have the vote.[18]

We must be careful, however, not to overemphasize class differences or construct over-elaborate interpretations of the data. Freedom-of-expression issues and the franchise are not among the most immediate concerns of Jalapans. Respondents readily answer questions about democratic practices, but there are no other indications that either those who support such practices or those who do not are personally disturbed about the local situation. On the contrary, as was shown in Table 5.1, there is near unanimity in all classes on the proposition that "any citizen who wishes to express himself on important local matters is free to do so." As we have seen, jobs, money, and urban services are really the focus of local attention, and if a member of the Communist Party or some other minority spokesman actually were to come to Jalapa to give a speech, one suspects that the essential tranquility of the city would not be greatly disturbed.

The prime importance of respondents' orientations toward democratic practices is thus found in the manner in which these orientations fit in with and reinforce other aspects of the political life of the city. As we have seen, Jalapa is a community appreciated by most of its citizens, but one where a large majority is deeply mistrustful of politics and politicians. It is a city in which

[18] In a suggestive chapter in his book on Venezuela, Frank Bonilla explores the extent of elite fears of masses thought to be "susceptible" and "available" to demagogic appeals. See "Elite Views of the Mass," Chapter 8, *The Failure of Elites* (The M.I.T. Press, 1970). Although we do not have comparable data and are dealing with a much broader sector of the population, Bonilla's analysis seems very close to our qualitative assessment of the Jalapan situation.

"Any citizen (including President Díaz Ordaz) who wishes
to express himself . . ."

most citizens view themselves as powerless to affect local decisions but think that they will be treated as well as (or no worse
than) others in encounters with police and bureaucrats. It is a
city in which contact with the existing political system tends to
increase negativism toward that system, but in which no opposition or reform movement exists to capitalize on the negativism.
Withdrawal, apathy, feelings of powerlessness, and indifference
to democratic practices form the dominant textures of citizen
orientations, interlaced with individual threads of self-esteem
and hope, feelings that one can and will somehow manage.

Thus, there are no masses struggling to free themselves in
Jalapa; there is no widespread sense of oppression or repression.
Those who are most deprived both economically and politically
are least involved in the political life of the community, orga-
nizationally, ideologically, and psychologically. Those who are
most advantaged are most active, allegiant, and satisfied. A long
learning process, reinforced by the elitist and bureaucratic nature of Mexican politics, has created a public that is on the one
hand negative toward politics and on the other hand uninvolved.
No identifiable cabal of chieftains or evil men is responsible for
the design or the results of this system. What we see in Jalapa is
an accretion of past practices, now rationalized by bureaucratic
methods, supported by those who are most advantaged, suffered

by those who are least advantaged, and eased by a national economy that has been more successful than many in generating opportunities and—in their absence—hope.

This is obviously not a fertile ground for reformers and agitators, for among a citizenry so negative about the everyday operation of the political system, every new aspirant to the public trust is automatically suspect, no matter what his expressed motives or goals. "More of the same" is the reaction of weary citizens. But this does not mean that the ring of institutions, behavior, and political orientations is irrevocably closed, or that the quiescence of the community can forever be taken for granted. People, institutions, and political practices are never in such perfect adjustment, not even in Jalapa. Thus, in the following chapter we shall reassess politics in the community from the larger perspectives of stability, change, and the future.

Six

The System in Balance and in Tension

The dominant theme of the last three chapters has been stability, or, as we would define it here, the propensity and capability of a system to restore itself to its original condition when challenged or disturbed by internally or externally generated forces. The public tranquillity and the absence of community conflict we observed in Jalapa are the outward face of a system that is relatively well tuned, self-balancing, and self-perpetuating. But if social science has not cautioned us against taking the stability of ongoing systems for granted, recent political events both in the United States and around the world should have reminded us that all political systems contain potentially destabilizing forces. To leave Jalapa without attempting some assessment, however tentative, of possible sources of tension and destabilization is to leave part of the job undone.[1] Before attempting this, however, it is necessary to summarize the ideas about stability that have been elaborated to this point.

Elements of Balance and Stability

Centralization and Control. The Mexican political system is not kind to politicians or ordinary citizens who are emboldened to

[1] Such unlikely events as a massive national economic reversal or the ascent to the Presidency of a radical leader would obviously be destabilizing throughout Mexico. But we are here concerned only with destabilizing forces and events that might be generated locally. Thus our analysis will focus on the possible emergence in Jalapa of groups or sectors of the popu-

practice their politics outside the institutionalized channels of government and Party. As was emphasized in Chapters 2 and 3, patterns of political recruitment and advancement and the manipulation of elections and other avenues of public expression make challenges to existing patterns of authority and to the substance of public policy difficult and therefore rare. The central authority's monopoly of rewards and sanctions (and its willingness to use both) makes such challenges costly for both elites and masses. In Jalapa, the monopoly is even tighter than usual, for the electoral competition found in some cities is unknown, and direct intervention by the governor is an ever-present possibility.

Historically, of course, there is no assurance that the centralization of authority and the monopolization of rewards and sanctions will guarantee public tranquillity. In the Mexican case, however, authoritarian practices have been leavened with sufficiently large dosages of flexibility and responsiveness to create a stabilizing mix.[2] From the point of view of most citizens, centralization and control are by no means absolute. Personal contacts, institutional representation, norms against the use of open coercion, and the widely recognized distinction between public and private affairs all soften and condition the arbitrary exercise of power. What remains characteristic of the system when all these other aspects are taken into account, however, is the extent to which the structure of political opportunity is restricted and the mechanisms of political recruitment are successful in excluding or transforming potential "troublemakers." Stability

---

lation that—because of their preferred values and patterns of behavior—might challenge ongoing ways of doing political business.

[2] Perhaps the best overall analysis of the sources of political stability in Mexico can be found in Roger D. Hansen, *The Politics of Mexican Development* (The Johns Hopkins Press, 1971), particularly Chapter 7, "The Peace of the PRI." Hansen emphasizes the system's capacity to (1) limit demands, (2) meet new demands that cannot be limited, (3) stimulate diffuse support, (4) retain specific support of those who are most relevant politically. Compare also the model of the modern corporation—which seeks to reduce competition, risk, and uncertainty through the control or stabilization of all relevant aspects of its environment—as developed by John Kenneth Galbraith, *The New Industrial State* (New York, 1967).

is thus in part the consequence of a set of practices that neutralize opposition on the one hand while exhibiting substantial responsiveness to cooperative petitioners on the other. Through the years, in Jalapa and elsewhere in Mexico, this game has been played subtly and successfully.

Managed and Restricted Participation. Patterns of participation in Jalapa are related to mechanisms of centralization and control, but they also have a dynamic of their own. As we have noted, elections are noncompetitive, and those who participate most in ways other than voting do so in a context that usually reinforces rather than threatens existing processes of decision-making and distribution. For example, urban improvements tend to go disproportionately to those neighborhoods most able to help pay for them. Market mechanisms are insinuated into the policy-making process, and richer citizens find themselves welcomed as participants in deliberations, whereas others are excluded. The central authorities invite participation, but on terms and occasions which they dictate and from which they hope to derive monetary or political benefits. For those who are already economically disadvantaged, political disadvantage follows in cumulative fashion.

As a rule, therefore, neither electoral nor other forms of participation are demand-generating or demand-multiplying. Of course the central authorities are on occasion pressured to respond to the petitions of citizens and groups, but these well institutionalized patterns of participation are very unlikely to get out of hand. In other words, very little uncertainty is generated by political participation in Jalapa. The outcomes of elections are known, the frequency and substance of particularistic and *ad hoc* demands are quite predictable, and participation in the design and implementation of public policies normally occurs—if at all—on terms set by the authorities themselves.

Even when uncontrolled participation occurs—for example, certain demonstrations and protests, refusal to pay taxes—the attendant uncertainty is usually transitory. If necessary, the state treasury and police are available to dampen protest, and lower officials and functionaries can always be sacrificed to appease an irate citizenry. The same authorities that manage participatory institutions in an attempt to ensure that all runs smoothly, have substantial reserves of men, money, and decisional power in case of trouble. The governor has great latitude in deploying these reserves. Thus, the potential for destabilizing political conflict is weakened at both ends: opportunities for the unrestricted expression of conflict-generating demands are minimized, and political situations that begin to develop unpredictable dynamics of their own very rapidly receive attention from higher authorities.

Groups, Classes, and Regime Interests. Because Jalapa has neither a large industrial sector nor extensive agricultural lands within its boundaries, it lacks two of the most common sources of political tension in Mexico. In this sense the city is somewhat unusual, for without substantial clashes of interest between labor and management or struggles over the ownership and use of land, the overall probability of conflict is definitely lessened. But in other respects the geography of potential conflict in Jalapa is not particularly different from that in the rest of Mexico.

In Jalapa as elsewhere, the PRI functions in part as an arena in which class, group, and individual conflicts can be handled without unduly upsetting the normal rhythms of political life. But perhaps more important is the extent to which the potential for sociopolitical conflict is attenuated by less formalized mechanisms. For example, there can be no doubting the degree of social structural inequality, differentiation, and variation in perspectives that prevails in Jalapa. Yet despite the diversity of political behavior, values, and attitudes, there are almost no significant organized expressions of class interests or class-based political movements in the city. The same is true, to a lesser extent, of group interests.

Why should this be the case? The reasons are many, and they have been elaborated at various places in this book. One in particular, however, warrants re-emphasis here. There is a shared investment in the existing regime that transcends class and group boundaries and interests. The reasons that lead the well-to-do and influential to attach themselves to the regime are quite different of course from the reasons that motivate the poor and marginal. For some, the key factor is the maintenance of positions of advantage; for others, the avoidance of life-disrupting conflict or of a worsened economic position. But whatever the motivation may be, the mutuality of interest in maintaining existing authority relations and preserving public tranquillity is considerable.[3]

Civic authorities assiduously cultivate an image of the dire consequences that might flow from allowing class, group, and factional interests full play in public life; and both the history of the Mexican Revolution and more recent attempts to democratize the Party give bite to their warnings about the Hobbesian potential of Mexican society. This point of view was clearly stated by a journalist-informant when commenting on local reform efforts: "There ought to be a change toward more municipal autonomy . . . but it ought to come slowly, not with one blow or *golpe,* not through a revolt . . . slowly, so as not to interrupt the institutional advances Mexico has made—advances that have cost so much blood and so many battles in the more than 50 years of the Mexican Revolution." Although there is no direct test of this proposition in our data, certainly civic order is one of the most universally valued commodities in Jalapa. In fact, there is evidence that those who are most marginally located in the social and economic structure value public order most of all. As emphasized in Chapter 5, the reluctance of lower-class Jalapeños to allow anti-PRIistas, Communists, and anti-Catholics to speak in the city derives not simply from their lack of

[3] J. David Greenstone defines a regime interest as "the stake that each citizen has—even if it is very small—in civil peace and in the particular pattern of public policy decisions or outputs that depend upon the stable, predictable capacity of the political authorities to obtain obedience readily." See "Stability, Transformation, and Regime Interests," *World Politics,* 22.3 (April 1970): 449–50.

appreciation for the importance of freedom of speech, but also from their appreciation of the historic fact that when agitators challenge existing institutions, the poor are usually the ones who suffer most.

The Legitimacy of Existing Practices. Like most discussions of Mexican politics, our analysis emphasizes the extent to which centralized and hierarchical forms of governance are accepted by the citizenry.[4] Although the behavior of politicians is frequently seen as corrupt and self-serving, and the operation of certain institutions is often viewed quite negatively, the tradition of strong, centralized, authoritarian rule is seldom challenged. However much citizens may be stung by individual experiences with centralized and arbitrary authority, they do not react by demanding that participation be democratized or that decision-making be decentralized.

Community-wide interest in the maintenance of public order is a partial explanation for public acceptance and legitimation of existing authority relations, but its roots are also to be found in the still-powerful tradition of Hispanic bureaucratic centralism. As suggested at the end of Chapter 2, the politics of Mexico —and especially of Jalapa with its state government and PRI monopoly—are living proof of the strength of that tradition and its capacity to adapt to and even to assume new institutional forms.

The logic that supports this conception of the proper way to organize political life argues that the central authorities must be both strong and well insulated from public pressures in order to encourage equity in administrative and distributive activities. Individual and group pressures are seen as "unbalancing" rather than as contributing to the justice and rationality of the process of governance. Opening the political process to widespread par-

---

[4] We are following Seymour Martin Lipset's definition of legitimacy as developed in *Political Man* (Garden City, New York, 1960): "Legitimacy involves the capacity of the system to engender and maintain the belief that the existing political institutions are the most appropriate ones for the society."

ticipation, competing interest groups, and citizen pressures is not considered justifiable either on moral grounds (as a right) or on empirical grounds (as a practice leading to greater equity).

Of course these arguments are not part of the conventional public dialogue in Jalapa, and it is doubtful that as abstract principles they would be embraced by most citizens. But many Jalapan institutions reveal the same assumption of acquiescence and passivity on the part of citizens that marked the ancient Iberian and Roman forms from which they have descended. The continuing legitimacy of the institutional tradition thus implies the acceptance of certain kinds of authority relations. Although some Jalapeños may consider themselves liberated from the thoughtways growing out of these elements in their Hispanic past, the community as a whole still gives strong support to the practice of—if not the original arguments for—centralized and hierarchical politics.

A parallel to the legitimation of political centralism is the acceptance of existing inequalities in the distribution of goods and opportunity. As emphasized in Chapter 4, Jalapeños, although in the main saying that the gap between rich and poor is too great, are nevertheless generally satisfied with the way they live and optimistic about the future. It would be misleading to say that the glaring social and economic inequalities of Mexico are themselves seen as legitimate (proper) by most respondents. On the other hand, when satisfactions and expectations are joined to other perspectives on economy and society, it can be said that there is very widespread acceptance of the socioeconomic status quo.

In general, these perspectives on society and economy contribute to the legitimacy of political institutions. As evidenced by the relationship between social class, education, views of the socioeconomic status quo, and political orientations, the citizen who is economically well situated, or at least satisfied—or who expects that one day he will be so—is not likely to call existing political arrangements into question. Moreover, what is asked of government is not that it be more responsive or open, but that it provide social, economic, and urban services that the private system of production and distribution does not seem to supply. To the extent that government performs reasonably well (in relation to expectations) as a supplier of such services, it is likely to remain quite acceptable to most citizens.

The tradition of centralized authority and the regime's ability to ride the coattails of socioeconomic satisfactions—while at the same time limiting expectations—certainly contribute to the legitimacy of existing political institutions. It is, however, a legitimacy that is much closer to a passive acceptance of the inevitable than to an intense belief in essential rightness. The extremely widespread negativism and cynicism noted in Chapter 5 are indicative of a citizenry very familiar with the uses of patronage and with the venality and elitism of city, state, and national politics. But the consequences of negativism and cynicism have been apathy and withdrawal, not opposition or reform movements that challenge the regime. The majority of Jalapeños may still believe that their political institutions are the "most appropriate ones for the society," but this is a belief rooted in political disillusion, narrowed perspectives, and restricted opportunities, not the more positive giving of support and affect that the concept of legitimacy is usually intended to convey.

The Depoliticization of the Community. One way of summing up the characteristics conducive to stability in Jalapa is to say that Jalapa is a depoliticized community.[5] Because of effective controls, restricted participation, fragmented social groupings,

[5] Depoliticization implies (1) a previously higher level of political involvement and (2) a systemic capacity to turn potential public-policy issues into mere problems of efficient administration. Throughout Mexico there is substantial evidence of this kind of long-term (post-Revolutionary) depoliticization, particularly as the managerial efficiency of the government/ Party apparatus increases. We emphasize the depoliticization of the community in the structural (second) rather than the individual (first) sense. These are obviously, however, two complementary perspectives on the same phenomenon. See Oscar Lewis, *Pedro Martínez* (New York, 1964); and Daniel Goldrich, "Political Organization and the Politicization of the Poblador," *Comparative Political Studies,* 3.2 (July 1970): 176–202.

and substantial legitimacy, there are notably few challenges, threats, demands, or uncertainties in local politics. In fact, there is not much local politics at all, if by politics is meant competition over the substance, perquisites, and benefits of public policy. There are, of course, the impressive management apparatuses of government and Party, and an elaborate political infrastructure including labor organizations, business associations, and other groups. Nevertheless, except for some busy and vocal careerists it can scarcely be said that Jalapeños have political life.

Even such seemingly intense political encounters as the occasional clashes over tax payments and project revenues are somewhat deceptive. They are examples of the process of control, implementation, and management gone wrong. They represent "defects" in administration rather than institutionalized participation in the formulation of public policy. Such confrontations, moreover, are usually absorbed into the public policy-making process without too much difficulty. They are thus not so threatening as they might seem at first glance. This absorptive process can be seen very clearly in a much more conflictual agrarian community in the neighboring state of Puebla:[6]

Such tough tactics [seizures, work stoppages] were reformist—not revolutionary or radical—in significance, despite any violence or anti-government overtones. . . . Direct-action tactics were just an essential part of the political game, and constituted institutionally accommodatable behavior which the government (and its police and military) were prepared to accept and manage. . . . The protagonists had most success when, given the mobilization of substantial popular and governmental support, they combined direct action with their bureaucratic lobbying. Indeed, the only way to achieve a major breakthrough was to resort to forceful direct action which created a public crisis.

In general, however, this technique of access through disruption is not much used in Jalapa.[7]

[6] David F. Ronfeldt, "Atencingo and the Politics of Agrarian Struggle" (unpublished doctoral dissertation, Stanford University, 1971), pp. 399, 401 (soon to be published by the Stanford University Press).

[7] As discussed in Chapter 3, university students are better situated and

A major structural factor related to depoliticization and the relative lack of political conflict in Jalapa is the fiscal and decisional weakness of the ayuntamiento. Widely perceived as impoverished and ineffectual, local authorities often receive what might be called political dispensation at the hands of the citizens. Instead of being attacked as a weak link in the hierarchy, or seized upon as a defenseless institution where political pressure might be applied with high chance of success, the ayuntamiento is often ignored. At the same time, authorities perceived as more relevant, whether in the Party or in the state government, are just that much more inaccessible, unaccountable, and experienced in managing and diverting demands. Thus, the weakness of local institutions does not encourage groups and individuals to enter the policy-making process. Rather, it makes entry into the political arena more difficult and conflict less likely.[8] In short, Jalapa is not an easy city in which to build a political fire. The critical mass of kindling is difficult to assemble, the wood is somewhat damp, matches are scarce, and the resident fire department is unusually efficient.

The withdrawal, apathy, negativism, and cynicism noted at many points in this study are both cause and consequence of depoliticization. Such orientations toward politicians and public life are reinforced by encounters with local and national institutions, in that, as we have seen, those who interact most often with public officials are the most negative toward politics and public officials. In any event, these deeply rooted orientations toward public life are themselves stabilizing elements. Disgust

---

equipped than any other group to use this technique and thus they command substantial respect among local politicians. Additionally, because the students have been able to sustain a public image of responsibility and public service (even when engaged in confrontation politics), they have been able to avoid the official repression and public hostility that normally accompany attacks on the political regime.

[8] This point is made as a general hypothesis by G. Bingham Powell, Jr., *Social Fragmentation and Political Hostility: An Austrian Case Study* (Stanford University Press, 1970), p. 106: "A system whose capability to act on a given issue is sharply restricted by factors beyond its control, and in which this lack of capability is generally recognized, is likely to face less political conflict on that issue than would a more capable system."

with political practices has not been translated into reformist movements, and apathy and withdrawal—although rational reactions to a situation in which resources are scarce, opportunities to participate restricted, and disadvantages cumulative—clearly smooth the way for centralized control and the management of potential conflicts.

The impact of this syndrome is multiple: There is a pervasive feeling that "government should do it," well documented in citizen responses to our questions about responsibility for solving Jalapa's major problems. Yet, except when particular conditions become unbearable for the individuals directly affected, there is little sustained effort to pressure public officials for improvements. Persons of substantial accomplishment are seldom attracted into public service, and the unimpressive officials who predominate do nothing to brighten the tarnished image of politics or to increase public trust. Ordinary citizens withhold energy and resources, remaining at the periphery of politics and public affairs, while viewing "agitators" with substantial hostility because they are likely to disrupt the smooth flow of public life.

Finally, there is a widespread disjunction between perceptions of private troubles and postures toward public policies. Although an overwhelming majority of citizens see Jalapa's most important problem as somehow the government's responsibility to solve, they do not translate these diffuse claims on the political system into effective demands. Additionally, the major source of personal difficulties—the economic situation and specifically the matter of jobs—is still widely perceived in the first instance as a private or individual domain. Individual mobility in the context of aggregate national growth is seen as the mechanism through which economic conditions will be ameliorated. A sense of personal blame and responsibility thus colors perspectives on these problems. For example, when Jalapeños were asked, "If a man is unemployed, who has the chief responsibility for finding work for him?" over 70 percent said that the man himself had that responsibility.[9] Despite substantial diffuse reliance on government, economics has not been connected with politics in ways that lead the average citizen to seek political redress for economic grievances.

Sources of Tension

Assuming that the organization and leadership of local politics remain much the same, is there nevertheless measurable potential for destabilizing sorts of change in Jalapa? Might attachment to the status quo weaken, perspectives on the proper role of government shift, and demands increase in ways that will make the governance of the community more problematical and difficult? More specifically, is it possible to discover attitudinal or value patterns that might presage the partial politicization of the community? Being careful always not to underestimate the complexity of the relationship among dissatisfaction, political awareness, and political action, let us search for such patterns.

Ascendant Sectors. Our primary ways of subdividing the citizenry in the search for potential sources of tension and change are by age, education, and class position. At the outset, we want to know whether sectors that are naturally on the ascendancy in Jalapa—by virtue of the passage of time and the spread of education—may in some sense be expected to rock the community boat. Do the young differ from their elders and the better educated from the less well educated in ways that suggest a growing potential for destabilization? Might existing socioeconomic policies be challenged and new demands be generated as the general level of educational attainment increases or as the young grow bolder and move into positions of more importance? Of

[9] Five percent of the respondents said "friends and relatives" and 23 percent mentioned the government or some other organization. The question was intentionally worded so as to direct attention away from the individual and toward "others." The lower a respondent is on the class hierarchy, the more likely he or she is to name "others"; class differences are not, however, great.

special interest is the potentially important sector of the population that is both young *and* well educated. Do these advantaged young people bear the seeds of new social, economic, and political orientations?

In order to investigate these questions without foundering in a sea of data and tables, we have adopted a strategy of comparative profiles of sectors of special interest. Using several questions and one index developed and presented in the past two chapters, we have examined how each of four sectors differs from a relevant comparison group among our respondents. Thus in Table 6.1, people under 30 (young adults) are compared with people over 30; educationally advantaged (beyond primary education) young adults are compared with other young adults; the educationally advantaged in general are compared with the educationally disadvantaged, and finally, people having at least some university education are compared with those having none.

The rationale for the selection of these four sectors has already been suggested. All of them are going to become more numerous and in some sense more important in the community. That the young will inherit Jalapa is a truism; those who are both young and educationally advantaged will contribute disproportionately to the community activists and elites of the next decades. The educationally advantaged sector will continue to grow as educational facilities expand, and—as has often been noted—the educationally advantaged are disproportionately active and important in other ways; the university group, with its special talents and expanding numbers, foreshadows what increased professionalization of community life might bring.[10]

[10] Initially, we intended to profile those who listed their occupations as "professional." The rationale was that there would be increasing demands for technical and professional skills in many domains of community life, coupled with increasing unwillingness of professionally trained people to accept the kind of politics practiced in Jalapa. Thus, this occupational group was hypothesized to be on the ascendancy both quantitatively and functionally, perhaps eventually forming the core of a reformist movement. We still support the original rationale, but since 90 percent of those with some university training list their occupations as "professional" and 90 percent

It was also decided that in these and subsequent profiles only men should be included. At numerous places in the previous chapters we have pointed out the marginality of women in community affairs, their more obvious withdrawal, their more intense conservatism, and their greater similarity to each other across class and educational lines. Just as it was necessary to document these sex-related patterns in order to understand the political culture of Jalapa, it is now necessary to recognize their implications for the analysis of potential sources of change. Briefly and bluntly, women do not count for much in the political life of the city, and if change does come, it is likely to be triggered and dominated by men.[11]

In Table 6.1, the variables are presented under two headings, the first having to do with personal satisfactions and expectations and the second bearing on more general social and economic issues. Each group is given a plus, a minus, or a zero rating according to the following coding rules: a group receives a plus if it differs from the one with which it is being compared in the direction of being more oriented toward the status quo, a minus if it is less oriented toward the status quo, and a zero if it does not differ significantly. Status-quo responses to questions grouped under the heading of personal satisfactions and expectations are those in which the respondent says he is satisfied, expects equal treatment, or expects to do well in the future.

---

of the professionals have at least some university training (the exceptions are some teachers), next to nothing is lost by presenting only the educational profile.

[11] Furthermore, to include women, whose attitudes and orientations range less widely than men's, is to lower the probability of finding significant differences between the sectors being compared. Most of the calculations and comparisons in Tables 6.1 and 6.2 would not, however, be overturned if women were included. We have also not presented comparative data on "perspectives on democratic practice" (see Table 5.8). The tendency for men and those with more education to be more open to speeches against the status quo and to extending the franchise to women and illiterates is not of great functional importance. In other words, no matter how fully Jalapeños were to endorse the rights of women, illiterates, and oppositionists (all guaranteed under existing legislation, anyway), nothing much would change in the community as long as other behavior patterns and orientations remained unchanged.

TABLE 6.1

Contrasted Profiles of Ascendant Sectors (Men Only)

Variable	Young *vs.* older men	Young, educationally advantaged *vs.* other young men	Educationally advantaged *vs.* other men	University-trained *vs.* other men
Personal satisfactions and expectations (Tables 4.7, 5.1, 5.5)				
General satisfaction with life	− −	+	0	−
Satisfaction with income	−	+	+	0
Sharing in national economic progress?	−	+	+ +	+ +
Sharing in national social progress?	−	+	+ +	+ +
Satisfaction with influence in Jalapa	− −	0	+	0
Expectation of economic betterment	+ +	+	+ +	+
Expectation of fair or equal treatment	+	0	+ +	+ +
Perspectives on economy, society, and change (Tables 4.7, 4.8, 4.9)				
Belief in national economic progress	+	−	+	−
Belief in national social progress	+ +	0	+ +	+
Attitude toward size of rich-poor gap	+ +	+ +	+	+
Belief in necessity of basic changes	0	0	0	+
Attitude toward land reform	−	+ +	+ +	+
Attitude toward expropriation of foreigners' property	− −	*amb.*	+ +	0
Attitude toward government control of economy	− −	0	+ +	+ +

NOTE: + + or − − means that Chi-square is significant at $p < .0001$; + or − means that Chi-square is significant at $.0001 < p < .05$; 0 means that Chi-square is not significant at the .05 level; *amb.* means that Chi-square is significant but the shapes of the two distributions being compared are so dissimilar that the interpretation of the difference is in doubt. "Young" is defined as under 30; "educationally advantaged" is defined as having at least some secondary education.

The highest N for each of the ascendant sectors profiled here (i.e. the largest number of responses for any item tabulated in a given column) is as follows: young men, 166; young and educationally advantaged men, 80; educationally advantaged men, 264; and university-trained men, 105.

Table numbers in parentheses following the two classifications of variables are those in which the variables listed below them were first presented.

For perspectives on economy, society and change, the status-quo responses are those suggesting that Mexico is doing well, that things are all right as they are, and that few if any changes are needed.[12]

As interesting as individual item and column comparisons might be, it is an overall comparison and interpretation of the profiles that most concerns us here. So as to keep in mind our emphasis on identifying bases for destabilizing changes in sectoral orientations, let us assess the profiles from what might be called a reformist perspective. What might those who would like to see a more egalitarian and progressive politics in Mexico reasonably hope for on the basis of the data in Table 6.1?

The first thing that would catch their eye is that the young men are "ahead" of the older men in several important ways (indicated by clusters of minuses in the profile). In all instances they are less well satisfied with their conditions of life, and they are much more likely to favor land reform, expropriation of foreign property, and government control of the economy. It would seem at first glance that this syndrome of greater dissatisfaction and propensity to embrace change bodes well for the reformist cause.[13]

A cautionary note, however should be sounded by the two clusters of pluses that appear in the profile of the young men. The first, having to do with expectations of economic better-

[12] As an example of how to read the table, consider "Satisfaction with income," the second variable under the heading "Personal satisfactions and expectations." The first minus indicates that young men are less well satisfied with their incomes than men over 30. The pluses in the second and third columns indicate that the educationally advantaged are better satisfied than those who are less advantaged, both among young men and also among men in general. The zero in the final column indicates that those with some university training do not differ significantly in satisfaction from those with no university training.

[13] It should be emphasized here that we are only pointing out tendencies that make change more probable. Our data will not support stronger inferences. Thus, no tight chain of causality is implied in our interpretation of the profiles. For example, the greater dissatisfaction observed among the young may well diminish as their incomes and conditions of life improve. Furthermore, it is difficult to infer from data of this sort the extent to which existing institutions and practices can fully accommodate the consequences of changed patterns of belief and perspective.

ment and fair treatment, suggests a group that although less well satisfied than its control group is nevertheless relatively optimistic about its present and future conditions. This counter-theme of optimism is reinforced by the data on perceptions of national economic and social progress. The young more frequently than their seniors see Mexico as doing well, and they also are less disturbed by the gap between rich and poor. The Mexican socioeconomic system continues to generate belief in its productive capacity and its essential rightness. Thus the overall profile is mixed. Considerable youthful dissatisfaction and openness to change coexist with relatively high expectations for the future and belief in the socioeconomic progress of the nation.

Although the aggregate profile of the young gives some modest cause for optimism from the reformist perspective, the profile of those who are both young and educationally advantaged dispels almost all these tentative hopes. If, as hypothesized, it is the educationally advantaged among the young who are going to be most important in the community of the future, then they are clearly less "promising" than their educationally disadvantaged peers. None of the trends among the young that gave rise to some hope for change are maintained among the educationally advantaged. Thus, economic and social satisfactions are higher among the educationally advantaged young than among those with less education. Similarly, the advantaged young do not embrace change-oriented programs as enthusiastically as do the disadvantaged. It would seem that as the young get more education, they become better satisfied and move toward the cultural center of gravity of the community. At times, in fact, the orientations that they hold approach positions of outright reaction. For example, on the question about the gap between rich and poor, 59 percent said that it was not big enough! Even when this is not the case, however, one gets a sense of young men who have been made quieter, more comfortable, and considerably better satisfied by their education.[14]

[14] There is little evidence in our data for anything that could be considered a politically meaningful generation gap. Authors who claim that such

The conservative pull of educational advantage is dramatically confirmed by the profile of all Jalapeño men who have a secondary or higher education. The column of pluses and double pluses suggests a group of citizens who can fairly be characterized as smug. From the reformist point of view, educational advantage is clearly the opiate of the masses. The tendencies already evident when the entire group of the young was considered are here writ large. If increasing educational opportunities continue to affect the orientations of the citizens as they have in the past, then there is no reason to predict that challenges to the status quo will arise. Quite to the contrary, the more defensible prediction is that existing orientations and expectations will merely be reinforced. The profile of those with university training does little to challenge this interpretation. Although the university-trained men are less well satisfied with life than other men and less confident of Mexico's economic progress, they are not a particularly promising group from the reformist viewpoint, either. In general they are relatively well satisfied and not particularly eager to see changes in existing public policies.

The Lower Class. Because of the high correlation between education and class, members of the sectors just discussed—with the exception of the young—come disproportionately from the upper and middle classes. The notion of ascendancy is clearly tied to educational advantage and class position. In general, our

a gap exists in Mexico—for example, Kenneth F. Johnson in his *Mexican Democracy: A Critical View* (Boston, 1971)—usually confuse student sentiment with youthful sentiment in general. In Jalapa there is no question that today's university students are less accepting of the status quo and more openly critical than either other young people or those who received their university training earlier. When age, education, and class are controlled, students at Veracruz University score higher than any other group studied on political activism, dissatisfaction with their present lives and with their political influence, and—particularly in certain facultades—supportiveness of social and economic change. For more detail see William Tuohy and Barry Ames, *Mexican University Students in Politics: Rebels Without Allies?*, Monograph Series in World Affairs, 7.3, University of Denver, 1970. However, none of these distinctive characteristics necessarily survives leaving the university, as data on those with university training who are now in the local work force suggest.

findings were that the most clearly ascendant sector of all, those who are both young and educationally advantaged, do not seem to hold values, orientations, or expectations likely to challenge the status quo. In fact, their orientations would seem to indicate a continuing reinforcement of the dominant textures of middle- and upper-class patterns of belief.

But Jalapa has another face, the apathetic and usually quies-cent lower class comprising almost half of the total population. Are there indications that this sector might one day become more of a problem than it now is?[15] Are trends such that lower-sector perspectives on self and system might lead to more in-volvement and increased demands? Do the young and the more advantaged among the poor loom as potential agents of change?

As will be recalled from Chapters 4 and 5, our survey finds the relative incidence of dissatisfaction, low expectations, and rejection of the status quo among lower-class citizens consis-tently higher than among middle- or upper-class citizens of Jalapa. Thus the lower sector is especially important in any discussion of potential sources of tension in the community. Of course, relatively greater numbers of lower-class Jalapeños are also withdrawn, cynical, and nonparticipant, and thus not now causing many difficulties for those who govern the city.[16] But this is potentially a conflictual configuration, particularly if op-portunities for the venting of grievances were to multiply. Thus

[15] Perhaps not even massive rural unrest would threaten political busi-ness-as-usual in Mexico so gravely as would a widespread change in the po-litical culture of the urban lower class. Neither the political system nor the economy is set up to handle the welfare and distributive demands that would ultimately ensue. The historic Mexican underclass tradition of "rising up angry" is, after all, an agrarian tradition. Politicians have experience in distributing land and using repression to quiet the countryside, but tech-niques for restabilizing the urban situation are neither so readily available nor so predictable in their effect.

[16] This is the common condition of the urban poor in the less developed nations. See, for example, Joan Nelson's "The Urban Poor: Disruption or Political Integration in Third World Cities?" in *World Politics*, 22.3 (April 1970): 393–414. Nelson concentrates on migrants, but much of what she says applies to the entire underclass. In her view, the most likely source of increased political importance for the urban poor is competition for their votes in multi-party systems where elections are important—clearly not probable in Jalapa or most of Mexico.

it is important to examine the orientations and expectations of the lower class in more detail.

The strategy adopted for this analysis is much the same as that used for the population as a whole. That is, we will isolate lower-class men, and then look at groups or sub-sectors among them. The basic expectation is that the world of lower-class Jalapeños is in many ways a microcosm of the larger society. The patterns of values, orientations, and perspectives that are dominant in the city as a whole should be reflected in the lower class. The range of differentiation is more restricted, but the consequences of stratification should be similar. To explore these possibilities among our survey respondents, Table 6.2 compares lower-class men earning between $40 and $80 a month with those earning less than $40 a month, those who are under 30 with those who are over 30, and the relatively few who have had some secondary schooling with those who have not. The group that is both young and educationally advantaged is too small to be analyzed statistically, and no one has any university training. In other respects, Table 6.2 is analogous to Table 6.1.

The first profile in Table 6.2 suggests that there is in fact a pattern of orientations within the lower class quite similar to that of the population as a whole. Those who have higher incomes and, we assume, better conditions of life are much less strongly oriented toward change and much more firmly convinced that they are sharing in Mexico's progress than are those who have the lowest incomes. The data are particularly striking with respect to perspectives on economy, society, and change. As mentioned in Chapter 4, no matter how poorly off these relatively advantaged members of the lower class may be when compared to members of the middle and upper classes, they are well aware that many others in the city are worse off than they are. They at least are usually wage-earning citizens who consume many modern products and can look back on a time when they or their families did not enjoy so many opportunities or amenities as they now have. They see themselves as having a stake in the status quo. This does not mean that they are necessarily

TABLE 6.2

Contrasted Profiles of Groups and Sectors Among Lower-Class Men

Variable	Higher-vs. lower-income men	Young vs. older men	Educationally advantaged vs. other men
Personal satisfactions and expectations			
General satisfaction with life	−	*amb.*	0
Satisfaction with income	0	− −	+
Sharing in national economic progress?	+ +	+	+
Sharing in national social progress?	+ +	−	+
Satisfaction with influence in Jalapa	− −	−	0
Expectation of economic betterment	−	+ +	+
Expectation of fair or equal treatment	+ +	+ +	+ +
Perspectives on economy, society, and change			
Belief in national economic progress	+ +	+	+ +
Belief in national social progress	+ +	+ +	−
Attitude toward size of rich-poor gap	+	+	0
Belief in necessity of basic changes	+	+	0
Attitude toward land reform	0	*amb.*	+ +
Attitude toward expropriation of foreigners' property	+ +	0	+ +
Attitude toward government control of economy	+	− −	+ +

NOTE: Symbols are explained in the note to Table 6.1. Total $N = 336$; highest N's of ascendant sectors respectively (left to right) = 168, 92, and 56. The young and educationally advantaged categories are defined as in Table 6.1; "higher" income here refers to an income between $40 and $80 a month as opposed to an income below $40 (500 pesos).

better satisfied than those who are poorer—as indicated by the minuses in their profile—but it does incline them to take relatively more conservative positions on many issues and to perceive themselves more often as sharing in Mexico's progress. Mexico's socioeconomic system in the main has been less harsh with them than with the poorest group; by casting their eyes downward, they see ample evidence of just how harsh it can be.

From this perspective of relative advantage, they are inclined to be less critical of existing arrangements and less prone to endorse change than their less fortunate fellow Jalapans.[17]

The profile of lower-class young men indicates a softening of the generational differences noted for the young in general. Whereas young men in the total population were clearly more change-oriented and less well satisfied than their elders, those of the lower class are only partially so. It should be remembered, of course, that in absolute terms lower-class young adults are still more dissatisfied and more strongly oriented toward change than their middle- and upper-class counterparts. In other words, the substantial differences between classes noted in previous chapters are not overridden. But when compared with older members of their own class, they are not so very different. More precisely, they differ at least as much in the status-quo direction as in the other, being in general more convinced than their elders that progress is being made, that changes are not needed, that existing economic differentiation is acceptable, and that their own conditions of life will improve. Perhaps these differences will be attenuated as their experiences with lower-class life-styles and possibilities become more extensive. But at present, relative to their own class, these young men do not seem a particularly angry or dissatisfied group.

Finally, the profile of the 17 percent of lower-class men who have some secondary education is quite revealing. Just as was the case for the population as a whole, educational advantage clearly increases acceptance of the status quo. With the single exception of perspectives on national social progress, those who have some secondary schooling are better satisfied, more hopeful of personal betterment, and less consistently oriented toward change than those who have no secondary schooling. This is a particularly impressive profile because, in terms of income, the educationally advantaged lower-class men are no better off

---

[17] As was the case for the population as a whole, the higher-income men of the lower class also more frequently report political contacts and a high sense of political efficacy than do those with lower incomes.

economically than those who are not advantaged: only half are in the higher-income group, and exactly half of those without secondary schooling are also in that group. Within the lower class, economic advantage does not cumulate with educational advantage as it does in Jalapa as a whole. Thus the relatively stronger status-quo orientations of the educationally advantaged lower-class men cannot be attributed to their more substantial economic positions. Education is operating independently to make them better satisfied and less oriented toward change than their less well educated brethren. The independent stability-enhancing effect of secondary schooling in Jalapa is nowhere more dramatically or more ironically documented than in this particular profile.[18]

In sum, the lower class shows only slightly less evidence than the upper and middle classes of the dynamic that characterizes Jalapa as a whole: increasing age, education, and income lead in the main to increasing satisfaction both with one's personal situation and with existing arrangements and institutions. This is not to claim that the more advantaged members of the lower class are sanguine about their prospects or conditions of life, but to warn against making unwarranted predictions about the potential for change inherent in lower-class perspectives on self and society when all else goes on as usual.

An Overview. These profiles, useful as they are as a basis for speculating about the future, nevertheless obscure the existing magnitude of differences among groups, sectors, and classes. We shall thus close this chapter by summarizing the distribu-

18 The irony is enhanced by the finding that lower-class men with some secondary education more often feel politically efficacious than do those with no secondary education, even though the former never qualify as politically advantaged, whereas the latter sometimes do. In *all* groups and sectors examined in Jalapa, the sense of political efficacy increases with education, no matter what the objective political possibilities or behavior of the group under consideration. Against the background of other orientations being considered, such an increase is probably most realistically interpreted as contributing to political stability. That is, a greater sense of political efficacy can be thought of as indicating increased satisfaction with one's political condition.

TABLE 6.3

*Incidence of Discontent, Openness to Change, Cynicism, and
Political Advantage in Jalapa*

(*Percent*)

Group or sector	Discontented ($N =$ 376/200)	Change-oriented ($N =$ 389/223)	Cynical ($N =$ 271/144)	Politically advantaged ($N =$ 257/232)
All respondents ($N = 1,556$)	24%	25%	17%	17%
Men ($N = 777$)	26%	29%	19%	30%
Women ($N = 779$)	23	21	16	3
Upper class ($N = 165$)	1%	5%	18%	36%
Middle class ($N = 587$)	16	20	15	20
Lower class ($N = 640$)	40	37	21	13
Men only				
Young adults ($N = 166$)	31%	24%	13%	30%
Educationally advantaged ($N = 264$)	16	20	13	36
Educationally advantaged young ($N = 80$)	19	21	21	21
University-trained ($N = 105$)	0	19	18	40
Upper class ($N = 98$)	0%	5%	20%	53%
Upper-class young ($N = 13$)[a]	0	0	15	0
Upper-class educationally advantaged ($N = 83$)	0	6	14	55
Middle class ($N = 295$)	12%	22%	12%	37%
Middle-class young ($N = 61$)	12	20	12	28
Middle-class educationally advantaged ($N = 104$)	14	23	7	46
Lower class ($N = 336$)	48%	43%	25%	21%
Lower-class young ($N = 92$)	48	30	13	35
Lower-class educationally advantaged ($N = 56$)	50	29	29	0
Members of the PRI ($N = 140$)	26%	28%	29%	66%[b]

NOTE: Each column heading is a classification based on one of our indexes. The larger N in each case represents all respondents so classified; the smaller, all men so classified. Appendix A compares the distribution of responses for Jalapa and urban Mexico in general to most of the questions on which the discontent and openness-to-change indexes (Columns 1 and 2) are based. This comparison finds Jalapans better satisfied with life but less well satisfied with their share of the nation's economic and social progress than the general urban population. Fewer Jalapans think the rich-poor gap is too large, but more support the expropriation of foreign property. In short, there is no consistent pattern of differences between the Jalapan and national samples. Probably if these two indexes could be fully reconstructed for a national sample (they cannot because of missing data), the proportions of discontent and openness to change would be found roughly equivalent in the two samples.

[a] Because of the extremely small N, the profile of the upper-class young should be interpreted with special care.

[b] Because membership in the PRI is one element in the index of political advantage, this percentage is artificially inflated.

tion of citizens who are discontented, change-oriented, cynical, and politically advantaged. Included in the presentation are not only those groups and sectors profiled in Tables 6.1 and 6.2, but others needed to complete the picture of the community as a whole. This overview, presented in Table 6.3, provides the data base for our final interpretation of sources of community stability and tension in the attitudes and perspectives of Jalapeños.

Table 6.3 maps the distribution of citizens who score high on four indexes: personal discontent, openness to change, cynicism about local politics, and political advantage. The indexes of discontent and openness to change are based on the two clusters of variables in Tables 6.1 and 6.2. The index of cynicism is constructed from five questions about politics and public officials in Jalapa.[19] The index of political advantage was introduced and used in Chapter 4. Note that the criteria of inclusion used are rather strict: only about one out of four Jalapeños is classified as discontented or change-oriented, and less than one out of five is classified as cynical or politically advantaged. The figures in each cell of Table 6.3 indicate what percentage of each class, sector, or group qualifies as having the characteristic in ques-

[19] These are simple summative indexes. For the index of discontent, one point was awarded for each of the following responses: dissatisfied with life in general; dissatisfied with income; not sharing in national economic progress; not sharing in national social progress. A respondent was considered discontented if he received three or more points out of a possible four. For the index of openness to change, one point was awarded for each of the following responses: the rich-poor gap is too big; favor an uncompensated land reform; favor an uncompensated expropriation of foreign property; government should control the entire economy. A respondent was considered change-oriented if he received two or more points out of a possible four (clearly an index that identifies individuals at the "radical" end of the change continuum). For the index of cynicism, one point was awarded for each of the following responses: the majority of officials in Jalapa are trying to advance their personal interests; it is useless to vote in municipal elections because leaders are pre-selected; a citizen of Jalapa wishing to express himself on important local matters is not free to do so; almost all decisions in Jalapa are made by a very small group of people; government in Jalapa is not doing everything possible to solve the most urgent problems. A respondent was considered cynical if he received four or more points out of a possible five (this index is specifically tied to items about Jalapa and is thus different from the scale of negativism previously used).

tion. For example, as shown in line four, of all members of the upper class, only 1 percent are discontented, 5 percent are change-oriented, 18 percent are cynical, and 36 percent are politically advantaged. The extent to which such a quantitative profile is "deviant" can be determined by comparing it with the profile of all citizens or with the profile of some other group or sector of interest.

The diverse data contained in Table 6.3 are not easy to summarize. Certain patterns, however, are quite clear. Discontent and, to a lesser extent, openness to change increase dramatically as one moves down the class hierarchy.[20] This is a reaffirmation of the findings presented at the end of Chapter 4. It is equally evident that class, not age or education, is the most important predictor of extreme discontent and openness to change.

On the other hand, the distribution of cynicism is relatively even throughout all groups and sectors examined. As noted in Chapter 5, certain basic perspectives on local politics (from which the cynicism index is constructed), are widely shared in the community. As was the case with the general scale of negativism toward politics, sex, age, education, and class are thus not particularly good predictors of cynicism; when those who are highest on the latter index are isolated, much the same uniformity of distribution occurs.[21] The relatively low level of extreme cynicism among middle-class men and the relatively high level among PRI members do, however, bear emphasis. The for-

[20] The clustering of discontent with openness to change is partially a class and partially an individual phenomenon. Among all respondents, the correlation between scores on the index of discontent and scores on the index of orientations toward change is .21. Among men only, the correlation is .25. When class is controlled, the partial correlations drop to .11 and .15 respectively. In general it is correct to say that those individuals who are most open to change are not usually those who are most discontented. This uncoupling of personal discontent or satisfaction and orientations toward change at the individual level further attenuates the destabilizing potential of these factors. If those who were most discontented were also more frequently those who were most open to change, the probability of political protest would be increased.

[21] See Chapter 5. The correlation between scores on the negativism scale and scores on the index of cynicism is quite high: for the population as a whole, $r = .47$; for men only, $r = .59$. The negativism scale and the cynicism index are obviously tapping much the same vein of orientations toward politics and the political process.

mer may reflect particularly strong taboos among members of the middle class against speaking out on such subjects, a reticence not so fully shared by members of the upper and lower classes. Of more interest is the ironic although not entirely unexpected finding that members of the PRI are disproportionately cynical about the conduct of local politics. Just as increased contacts with politics lead to higher levels of negativism among the population as a whole, the "richer" political life of PRIistas leads them to be numbered more frequently among the ranks of the extremely cynical. When class is controlled, PRIista men look very much like the population of all men on most questions involving orientations and perspectives on self, society, and economy. Thus, their relatively higher levels of cynicism seem to relate directly to their higher levels of involvement in the political life of Jalapa rather than to other orientations and perspectives. Other Jalapeños of similar class or educational background can probably more easily avoid confronting the gap between idealizations and political reality.

Finally, the distribution of political advantage reconfirms and extends the analysis made in Chapter 4. Women are practically never among the advantaged; and among the men, educational advantage and thus more conservative political positions are positively related to political advantage (except in the lower class). In general, the more advantaged a group, sector, or class is, the less discontented and change-oriented it is likely to be.

In sum, the data in Table 6.3 suggest—as have the data in the previous two chapters—a population in which there is substantial personal discontent and openness to change, but in which these feelings are concentrated among those who are also least motivated and least able to enter into political activity. When viewed in isolation, such levels of discontent and change-orientation might seem to presage a bubbling up of destabilizing demands for services and benefits in the future. Even the substantial degree of cynicism might seem to be eventually transmutable into demands for political reform. But before such demands could emerge, there would have to be a significant broadening

"*Just between us, as militants of the same party, who's your candidate?*"

of structural and institutional opportunities for participation as well as heightened perceptions of the relevance of politics to one's personal condition. We have no evidence that the institutions or citizens of Jalapa are changing in this way. In fact, opportunities may even be narrowing as institutions are ever more effectively managed. Moreover, the costs of serious protest in Mexico (for those few who might be considering it) are great, as students and young people have so recently been reminded.[22] In view of this complex of factors, it would be rash indeed to predict that discontent and openness to change will easily or quickly be translated into destabilizing political forces in cities like Jalapa.

[22] On June 10, 1971, the first major student demonstration in Mexico City since the protests, marches, meetings, and killings of late summer, 1968, took place. During this demonstration, the marchers were attacked by about five hundred well organized, club- and gun-wielding "irregulars," mostly young and widely thought to be in connivance with the police who stood silently by—along with 3,000 paratroopers—while the battle raged. Semi-official reports set the number of demonstrators killed at 11, while student leaders estimated 27 dead and 22 missing. The attackers used bamboo staves, pistols, and semi-automatic rifles on the crowd, and also entered at least one hospital, beating wounded students and preventing doctors from treating them. President Luis Echeverría subsequently blamed the attack on "mercenaries connected with inferior authorities," and the mayor of Mexico City resigned. See the summary report in the *New York Times*, June 20, 1971, section 4, p. 3.

Seven

Perspectives on Politics

The achievements of the Mexican regime cannot lightly be brushed aside. Not only is the aggregate economic growth that has been achieved over the past three decades impressive, but contemporary political arrangements are a real improvement over much that existed before the Revolution. As political monopoly replaced political free enterprise, the old ruthlessness, the old reliance on open coercion, and some of the most striking forms of social and economic exploitation were replaced or moderated. The average Mexican, whether urban or rural, lives in a more secure political and economic environment than did his father or grandfather, and in relation to many other Latin Americans he is demonstrably better off.

Yet something is very wrong in Mexico. Pyramiding privilege, manipulation, corruption, poverty, apathy, and negativism abound in Jalapa and the rest of the nation. These are not just the expected imperfections of a regime struggling against an obdurate environment, but rather the ugly other side of the Mexican developmental model—the costs, it might be said, of *el milagro mexicano.* Neither from the perspective of the self-imposed standards and goals of the Mexican revolutionary ideology nor in terms of more general formulations of the good society are these costs fully acceptable.

Thus at many points in this book we have adopted a critical posture toward the Mexican political regime. These criticisms suggest a normative model against which the institutional arrangements and performance of the regime are being measured and evaluated. It is time to make this model more explicit.

The model derives from three tenets of classical democratic theory: the common man ought to participate in the making of those decisions that most directly affect him; there ought to be ways in which those who rule can be called to account by those who are ruled; the government ought to ensure that available resources are distributed in a reasonably equitable manner, particularly those goods and services necessary to basic human welfare. In all three of these regards the Mexican regime is found wanting.[1]

Participation in Policy-Making

If ordinary men and women in Mexico were not only allowed but actually encouraged to come together to help shape the decisions that affect their lives, the effect would be staggering. Not only would there be a veritable explosion in political participation at the local level, but there would also be profound changes in the style and distribution of participation.[2] Recall that after ritualized voting the most common political activity in Jalapa (engaged in by only 20 percent of the population) was "going to an official to seek help." This is the classic posture of the petitioner, hat in hand before a bureaucrat. These individual and

[1] The welfare and distributive criterion is not always included in discussions of democratic theory. Nevertheless, as we hope previous chapters have made clear, questions of welfare and distribution in Mexico are directly related to issues of participation and elite accountability. Thus, for our purposes, all three should be considered together. See David Braybrooke, *Three Tests for Democracy: Personal Rights, Human Welfare, Collective Preference* (New York: 1968). We have also found the work of Robert Dahl, Henry S. Kariel, C. Wright Mills, and C. B. MacPherson useful.

[2] In discussing participation (and to a lesser extent in discussing the relationship of leaders and led) we shall limit ourselves to the local level even though what we say has implications for national politics. Policy-shaping participation of the kind we are talking about is much easier to imagine and put into effect in relatively small-scale environments. Minimal requirements of citizen information, preparedness, and perceived self-interest are more easily met.

often *post-facto* attempts to win exemption from a decision already made or special consideration from the centralized political-administrative apparatus, hardly meet the norm of rank-and-file participation in the formulation of policy.

Furthermore, those relatively infrequent acts (participation in organizations, the Party, and political campaigns) that seem at first glance to be more genuinely contributory to the shaping of policy are found wanting when examined in detail. The Mexican style of political mobilization and participation is integrative and extractive in both intent and consequence. It serves to channel energies into those activities that are necessary to maintain existing practices and institutions.

Any movement toward increased participation in the shaping of policy implies a profound redistribution of political opportunity and thus of political power. If Jalapa is a fair indication of the situation in the rest of Mexico, all varieties of participation, whether potentially policy-shaping or not, are disproportionately the province of the affluent and the educated. Recall that members of the upper class and men in particular are disproportionately represented in the local PRI. The formally sanctioned system of corporate or sectoral representation is bypassed and subverted by an informal system of individual and interest-group representation that tends to concentrate power in the hands of people who are already relatively well located in the society and in the economy. In short, the pyramid of Party power is not nearly so distinct from the pyramid of social and economic privilege as its supporters claim. The Party in general is thus not an arena in which the dispossessed, those who because of their socioeconomic station normally enjoy neither easy access to nor adequate representation in their government, can regularly be heard. Furthermore, as was noted in Chapter 4, the actual situation of the lower class outside the Party is even worse than the model of pyramiding inequality would indicate. Education and political advantage are positively related to each other among members of the upper and middle classes, but negatively related in the lower class. Ironically, what is a resource at the upper end of the class hierarchy is irrelevant or a liability at the lower end. In rural areas, the situation is undoubtedly even more acute.

The reluctance of the managers of modern Mexico to grant public access to the policy-making process reflects not only their fear of "the chaos latent in the mass,"[3] but also more specific concerns. Substantially increased participation would shatter the agenda-setting monopoly now enjoyed by the inner circle of the government/Party apparatus and their cohorts in the industrial sector. For example, if the lower sectors of society were genuinely represented in the policy-making process, it is difficult to believe that beautification of the central plaza could long continue to take precedence over improved drainage and pavement in the *barrios humildes*. The poor might not see their priorities as planners and technocrats would. They might prefer a soccer field to a new classroom. But they know when their feet and floors are wet and surely would not long tolerate an agenda on which their needs, however they might be perceived, came near the bottom.

The fragmentation and privatization of problems that characterizes citizen perspectives on politics in Jalapa would also diminish under conditions of increased participation. By coming together in the process of trying to influence policy, economically and politically deprived people would find themselves voicing common problems and similar views. Those who are currently most isolated from each other—and victimized in their isolation—would learn that there are alternatives to the role of "subject." What would thus eventually be anticipated is nothing less than a general rise in political and class consciousness. Expectations about the responsibilities of government and criteria by which the performance of government is judged would change. The often-repeated assertion that government has the responsibility for solving community problems now seldom connotes more than a diffuse feeling that if *el gobierno* does not do

[3] The phrase is Frank Bonilla's in *The Failure of Elites* (Cambridge, 1970), p. 127.

it, no one will. This is quite different from widespread consciousness that a man's problem is also his neighbor's, and that only
in concert with others can the common man possibly hope to
have political influence.[4]

Thus, the scattered citizen energies that now go into feather-
ing individual nests and guarding against the intrusions of the
bureaucratic state would coalesce in an organizational sub-
structure that would be much harder for the government/Party
apparatus to manage. Widespread participation in the policy-
making process makes the playing off of one petitioner against
the other and the distribution of rewards and opportunities
along patronage lines much more difficult. Of course such practices would continue, but they would not dominate to the extent that they now do.

The Leaders and the Led

Accountability implies more than sensitivity to public preferences; it implies mechanisms by which those in positions of political and administrative power can be called upon to explain
and justify their behavior and can be removed if substantial
numbers of people feel that they have exercised their decisional
prerogatives poorly or inappropriately. Of course the norm of
accountability does not give specific content to "poorly or inappropriately," nor does it specify any meaning for "substantial
numbers of people."[5] But at least it directs attention to the key

[4] An example might be the question of unemployment, now widely perceived as a problem, but highly privatized in terms of solutions. As noted
in Chapter 6 above, a large majority of citizens see "the man himself" as
having the responsibility for finding a job when he is unemployed.

[5] More formally, it does not even begin to answer the enduring questions raised in all serious discussions of accountability. Accountable to
whom—to future generations yet unborn, as Burke would have it? Who is
accountable—the corporate and educational apparatuses as well as the political and administrative officials? Accountable for what—for the *n*th un-
foreseeable consequence of every decision? In the Mexican case, however,
almost no officials are made to answer for anything by anyone except their
superiors in the government/Party apparatus to which they themselves
belong. This system of elite self-legitimation is what concerns us here, not
the philosophical and empirical issues raised by pressing against the boundaries of the accountability problem.

question of control over the behavior of officials through institutionalized capacity to sanction.

Elections are usually thought to be the most legitimate and effective way of guaranteeing accountability. The theory of electoral accountability has become the last refuge for those who see no other way in which the masses can realistically exercise control over their governors. Given the prevalence of public apathy and ignorance, the unequal distribution of resources and opportunities, the complexity of most public policy controversies, and the bureaucratization of decision-making, electoral defeat—or in rare instances electoral recall—is viewed as the ultimate (and often the only) general sanction on leaders who do not so markedly violate community standards as to land in jail.

But there is a multiple irony in the concept of electoral accountability as applied to Mexico. In the first place, the very factors that make elections the last hope for citizen control over decision-makers subvert the possibility of such control. Where apathy, ignorance, unequal distribution of resources, complicated policy issues, secrecy, and bureaucracy define the common condition, elections can make little difference. Political elites are already assured almost complete autonomy from the rank and file in their decision-making, and the threat of an election some years hence—an event touching only a minority of them and one they can manipulate to a substantial degree in any case—is hardly a real check on authoritarianism and unresponsiveness in office. In the second place, the noncompetitive nature of Mexican elections and the no–re-election rule violate the basic premises on which the hope of electoral accountability rests. Where there is no real public competition for office and where a politician never has to face the people who elected him to answer for his sins in office, the hypothesized structure of institutionalized constraints crumbles.

Yet it is precisely in the spirit of the theory of electoral accountability that most criticism and proposed reform of the PRI and the Mexican party system are put forward. The ill-fated Madrazo experiment in democratizing the Party would have introduced competitive primaries into the nomination process.[6] Madrazo and other reformers have insisted that increased competition for public office would be salutary. But salutary for whom and for what? If the spoils of political office more frequently went to PANistas would they be likely to behave much differently as incumbents than PRIistas? Would PRIistas adjust their behavior in the light of countervailing party power and the threat of electoral defeat? Within the PRI would knowledge that nomination depended on ratification by a larger clientele necessarily inhibit or control behavior in office?

Without doubt, increased competition for office both inside and outside the Party would provide opportunities for new voices to be heard, for opposition to be expressed, and for seignorial rights to be challenged. Autocratic and centralized control would diminish somewhat, and the spoils of office would be more evenly divided. These are important changes. Indeed if they did not mark so many sacred cows for slaughter, they would not be so widely and effectively resisted. But the search for mechanisms of accountability drives one even more deeply into the structure and functioning of the regime, for no amount of competition within or between parties can by itself effectively control the behavior of officials once safely in office. Other conditions would have to change as well.

In the first place, the underrepresentation and malrepresentation of certain groups and sectors within the PRI would have to end. The criteria whereby candidates are now assessed are naturally those most meaningful to the dominant members of the Party, and those chosen are naturally obligated to the groups

[6] Although the Madrazo experiment was primarily concerned with competition in the context of nominations for public, elective office at the municipio level, the arguments in its favor are even stronger when applied to offices within the Party. The dominant position of the Party makes its internal and sectoral staffing properly matters of public concern, but its officials are even more insulated from the public than government officials. For a study of one attempt (a failure) to open up the nominating process for such offices (in this case, the head of the League of Agrarian Communities in Veracruz), see William Tuohy and David Ronfeldt, "Political Control and the Recruitment of Middle-Level Elites in Mexico: An Example from Agrarian Politics," *Western Political Quarterly*, 22.2 (June 1969): 365–74.

and factions supporting them. Unless real democratization of party membership and participation takes place, the only change will be to substitute competitive elitism for controlled elitism. This is precisely what happened during the Madrazo experiment. Groups competing for the spoils of office disrupted the orderly political process, and no noticeable advantage accrued to those who were disadvantaged under the old system. Certainly officials did not seem perceptibly more inclined to take their obligations as public servants seriously.

In the second place, there would have to be more opportunities for citizens to review the performance of both Party and government officials. Whether by opening up many appointive positions to rank-and-file nomination and scrutiny, or by holding Party-sponsored public grievance sessions during which officials would face their clients, the cutural and institutional factors that insulate the leaders from the led would have to be stripped away. The elite bias of the current system of internal validation, whereby officials are answerable only to their superiors—and wherein whitewashing, with an occasional low-level sacrifice, is the norm—would have to be reversed.

To suggest such changes, however, is to be reminded of their difficulty, for the Party/government apparatus is both at the heart of the problem and, in the short run, perhaps the only arena in which solutions can be explored. Yet the men who run this apparatus, who use it to service the executive branch and advance their own career ambitions, are well aware of the ramifications of such changes: increased political conflict, uncertainty and risk in situations that are now predictable and safe, reduced patronage, and reduced opportunity for self-aggrandizement. Precisely because these ramifications are so clearly seen, change will not come easily.

Distribution and Welfare

In the short run, increased public participation in decision-making would change the distribution of benefits in Mexico. What Roger Hansen wryly calls the *real* Mexican miracle—that Mexico's economic policies have fueled the growth process, while its

political system has successfully absorbed the pressures resulting from the impact of rapid growth on demands for welfare—
would begin to fade.[7] If restrictions on participation were re-
laxed, self-interest would soon lead deprived sectors to push
harder in the competition for social and economic benefits. It
is probable also that demands for increased benefits would out-
run supply, at least for some goods and services. Thus, increased
political conflict is implied by the participatory, competitive
dynamic.

But in the long run, those who feel threatened by the rise of
new claimants are in a very strong position not merely to defend
their interests, but to counterattack. When such attacks are successful, unbridled competition may eventually lead to greater
inequity of distribution. Furthermore, in poorer countries like
Mexico, empowerment usually takes place so unevenly that
large sectors of the population are left outside the competitive
game entirely, consigned to the leavings of a "trickle-down" system. Their share of aggregate economic growth is small or negli-
gible, thus deepening the gulf that already separates them from
the rest of society.

The insufficiency of competition in the long run as a mechanism for increasing social justice and assuring an equitable distribution of economic benefits is reinforced by the nature of the
benefits usually sought. Common-sense views of welfare in the
twentieth century typically emphasize the need for adequate
food, clothing, shelter, medical care, and education. Such additional benefits as safety and congenial employment are also
sometimes included.[8] Many of the physical and institutional facilities needed to increase welfare must necessarily be provided

[7] Roger D. Hansen, *The Politics of Mexican Development* (The Johns
Hopkins Press, 1971), p. 4.

[8] See the list in Braybrooke, p. 129, and compare the analysis (based
on Mexican census categories) in James W. Wilkie, *The Mexican Revolution: Federal Expenditure and Social Change Since 1910* (Berkeley: 1967),
Chapters 9 and 10. Implied in our discussion, as in Braybrooke, pp. 121–
45, is the view that such a list has more or less universal validity and should
take precedence over mass preferences—whether for soccer fields, leisure,
bread, or circuses—in defining and evaluating welfare.

by the state. Neither individuals in competition with each other nor the private sector in competition with itself or with the state can provide the schools, hospitals, sewage systems, water supplies, roads, markets, and bureaucratically dispensed services that are needed.

The issues of welfare and its distribution thus come inevitably to depend on the commitment and the capacity of political elites to design and carry out programs truly conducive to increasing equity. Leadership, not just grudging responses to demands, is called for. It is precisely here, however, that Mexican elites are most vulnerable to criticism, for despite a firm constitutional obligation and an oft-repeated rhetorical commitment to welfare measures, their performance has not been impressive. To some extent this lackluster performance can be blamed on scarce resources, but even within the bounds set by scarcity, much more could be done. How is this lack of real commitment shown?

In the first place, development is always a question of the purposes to which national resources and energies will be put, and when these resources and energies are scarce, the competition for them is intense. In Mexico the proponents of public health facilities and schools find themselves in a very unequal bargaining position as opposed to the backers of other kinds of national investments (whether massive hydroelectric projects, airport improvements, the beautification of Acapulco). Elaborate economic and technical justifications for these latter kinds of public works have been devised, but these justifications cannot fully hide the fact that important human choices are also being made. Superhighways to the sea? Irrigation systems? Facilities for the Olympic Games? "Development for whom?" is an embarrassing question and thus not often asked. Priorities are tacitly set according to criteria derived from a model of maximum aggregate economic growth and national prestige that underplays or denigrates "nonproductive" investments in welfare.

In the second place, elites fail to take the measures necessary to increase the probability that welfare benefits will reach those

who need them most. One of the most critical lessons taught by
the Cuban revolution is that even when elite commitment to
equitable distribution of benefits is above question, and aggregate investment in welfare is greatly increased, improvements
in schools, clinics, sanitation, housing, and diet do not flow naturally to poorer and more isolated regions. The teachers, doctors,
nutritionists, engineers, or construction workers who transmit
the new benefits do not automatically or joyfully commit themselves to working in the areas and environments where they are
most needed. Networks of transportation and communication
must be set up to sustain the flow of men and materials on which
programs depend. Self-reinforcing patterns of culture and behavior often have to be modified before those who need the
benefits most can come to accept them and incorporate them
into their way of life. In short, in Mexico as elsewhere, increased
equity in the distribution of welfare benefits always goes against
the currents of economy, culture, and society. Delivery systems
must therefore be designed to *drive* benefits upstream against all
the human and material obstacles that stand in their way. It is
one of the many paradoxes of the developmental drama that
there is necessarily an autocratic and centralized component to
this egalitarian effort. And it is one of the most glaring shortcomings of the Mexican regime that it uses its autocratic and centralized decisional capacity so much more willingly to preserve
existing privilege than to achieve social justice.

The glories, the horrors, and perhaps even the flickering
dreams of the Mexican Revolution are dead. That thirty-year

explosion of violence, hopes, fears, destruction, and reconstruction no longer resounds in the land. In its place is a well oiled political and economic machine run by an elite committed to maintaining itself and to furthering national development defined as movement toward a modern industrialized society. In the name of such development, the cooperation of public, private, and foreign capital is sought and a multitude of obvious sins are excused.

But there are other visions of development, progress, and the good society, articulated not only by utopian philosophers but also by the violent and blood-stained men who fought their way to prominence in the Mexico of Villa and Zapata. These are visions in which *justicia social* is central, in which the common man is viewed as the beneficiary rather than the means of national development. However flawed or difficult to realize these visions may appear to be when examined in detail, they contain an irreducible component of truth: The arrangements that enable a nation to become rich and powerful are not necessarily those most conducive to improving the quality of life of its citizens. Even if material needs are eventually more equitably met —and Mexico shows that this is by no means inevitable—a wide range of other human needs remains.

The costs of neglecting this alternative vision of development are borne not only by millions of Mexicans but also, if only indirectly, by others in search of viable and life-enhancing pathways out of poverty and underdevelopment. Mexico, because of its revolutionary background and impressive post-Revolutionary economic growth, is inevitably held up as a model. Yet what has it to teach? That social justice has to be sacrificed to aggregate growth? That the countryside must be neglected in favor of the city? That the commercialization of culture and economy is an inevitable result of prosperity? That greed, corruption, and mass manipulation are the earmarks of leadership? That apathy, negativism, and withdrawal are the common condition of citizens? That the expression of grievances ought to be met with gunfire, beatings, and jail when more ordinary controls fail? Is this the necessary and enduring legacy of the Mexican Revolution? We hope not. Yet it is not our place to carry advocacy further. Beyond our relatively cautious prescriptions about participation and welfare, alternative visions ought to come from the principals themselves, Jalapeños and other Mexicans. Perhaps a new generation of patriots will one day demonstrate to a doubting hemisphere that in the land of Zapata, when men and women take action to translate flickering dreams into reality, innovation in politics and economics is still possible. We hope so, and we wish them well.

Appendixes

Appendix A
Comparisons Between Jalapa and Urban Mexico

The comparative data on urban Mexico used here were taken from the three sources described below. All three are national samples drawn from urban areas having more than 10,000 inhabitants, and in all three the sample was stratified according to city size and geographical location, with blocks, households, and respondents in each city chosen on a random basis. In the tabulations that follow, the "Mexico" data will be from *The Civic Culture* unless otherwise noted.

Gabriel Almond and Sidney Verba, *The Civic Culture* (Princeton University Press, 1963). Original sample size 1,008; weighted sample size 1,295. Data available through Inter-University Consortium for Political Research, University of Michigan.

"A Barometer Study of Mexican Public Opinion" (Roper 1), conducted by International Research Associates for the United States Information Agency in January 1961. Original sample size 1,107; weighted sample size 1,479. Data available through the Roper Public Opinion Research Center, Williams College.

"A Barometer Study of Mexican Public Opinion" (Roper 2), conducted by International Research Associates for the United States Information Agency in September and November 1961. Original sample size 1,067; weighted sample size 1,511. Data available through the Roper Public Opinion Research Center, Williams College.

Category	Jalapa	Mexico
Social Class		
Upper	9%	11%
Middle	41	43
Lower	50	46
Age		
20–29	25%	35%
30–39	26	27
40–49	23	17
50 or over	26	21
Education		
None	16%	20%
Primary	59	65
Secondary	17	12
Some university	8	3
Occupation[1]		
Professional, executive, managerial	12%	5%
Sales and clerical	18	22
Small business	17	14
Skilled labor	22	41
Farm or manual labor	25	14
Domestic service	6	3
Monthly income		
Less than 500 pesos	33%	41%
500–999 pesos	30	25
1,000–7,999 pesos	37	33
8,000 pesos or more	—	1
Organizational membership		
None	67%	75%
One	18	23
Two	11	2
Three or more	4	—
Membership in a political organization (for those who belong to organizations)		
Yes	42%	48%
No	58	52
Party membership		
PRI	11%	7%
Other	—	1
None	89	92
Have tried to influence a decision		
Often	1%	1%
Once or twice	3	5
Never	96	94

Category	Jalapa	Mexico
How much economic progress in Mexico?[2]		
A great deal	58%	42%
A little	32	48
Almost none	5	6
None	5	4
Are you benefiting from this progress?		
A great deal	11%	12%
A little	38	57
Almost none	16	13
None	35	18
How much social progress in Mexico?		
A great deal	51%	44%
A little	37	47
Almost none	5	5
None	7	4
Are you benefiting from this progress?		
A great deal	15%	20%
A little	37	55
Almost none	12	9
None	36	17
Satisfied with life?[3]		
Well satisfied	31%	5%
Satisfied	47	51
Dissatisfied	16	33
Highly dissatisfied	5	10
How will your economic situation change in the next ten years?		
Get better	65%	70%
Stay the same	21	19
Get worse	14	11
Opinion on size of rich-poor gap[4]		
Much greater than it should be	37%	71%
Greater than it should be	21	12
About right	25	13
Less than it should be	18	4
Are basic changes necessary?		
Yes	85%	90%
No	15	10

[1] Housewives are omitted here.
[2] Data on urban Mexico here and in the next three items are from Roper 2.
[3] Data here and in the last two items of the comparison (p. 177) are from Roper 1.
[4] Data in this and the basic-change item are from Roper 2.

Category	Jalapa	Mexico	Category	Jalapa	Mexico
Opinion on land reform			Opinion on expropriation		
Oppose	16%	19%	of foreigners' property		
Favor, but compensate in full	26	23	Oppose	29%	45%
Favor, but compensate in part	49	52	Favor, but compensate in full	12	11
Favor, but no compensation	9	6	Favor, but compensate in part	39	35
			Favor, but no compensation	20	9

Appendix B
Questionnaires Used in Jalapa

The Citizen Questionnaire

Good day (afternoon). We are making a study of public opinion for a large university in order to find out what the people of Jalapa think. We are interested in local problems as seen by those who live here, and we are particularly interested in *your* point of view. For this purpose we would like to ask your collaboration in the present survey. We would appreciate your help in this: please let us ask you some questions that we are also asking in many other parts of the city.

1. How long have you lived in Jalapa?[1]

2. In your opinion what are the most urgent or serious problems that affect Jalapa?

3. (Ask if more than one problem is mentioned in Item 2.) Which of Jalapa's current problems preoccupies you most, personally?

4. Who do you think has the responsibility for solving this problem?

5. Can you yourself do anything to solve this problem?

6. Speaking of the local problems here in Jalapa, how well can you understand them—very well, well, more or less, or not at all?

7. Suppose a law or regulation that you considered very unjust or prejudicial to your interests or to the interests of people like yourself were being considered by the municipal government of Jalapa. Do you think you could do anything about it?

8. If such a case actually arose, how probable is it that you would really do something to try to change it—very probable, probable, improbable, or completely improbable? (If the respondent says "Completely improbable," skip to Item 10.)

9. If you were to make an effort to change this law or regulation,

---

[1] Response categories to many closed questions are either shortened or omitted entirely here.

how probable is it that you would be successful—very probable, probable, improbable, or completely improbable?

10. Suppose there were some question that you had to take up with one of the government offices here in the city—do you think you would be treated in the same manner as any other person? (If the respondent says "No," ask whether he thinks he would be treated better or worse.)

11. If you tried to explain your point of view to officials of that office, do you think they would pay a great deal of attention to you, pay a little bit of attention to you, or ignore you completely?

12. If you had some trouble with the police—for instance, if you were accused of a minor infraction—do you think you would be treated in the same manner as any other person, or not? (If the respondent says "No," ask whether he thinks he would be treated better or worse.)

13. If you tried to explain your point of view to the police, do you think they would pay a great deal of attention to you, pay a little bit of attention to you, or ignore you completely?

14. Would you like to have more influence in community affairs, or are you satisfied with the influence that you now have?

15. Do you think the government here in Jalapa does everything possible to solve the most urgent or serious problems that affect the city, or not?

16. Do you think the responsibility for solving the common problems of Jalapa rests exclusively with public officials, or not?

17. Do you think the majority of public officials in Jalapa are trying to help the community in general or trying to advance their personal interests?

18. Although Jalapa may not be perfect, I think it offers just about everything a person could want. Is this true or not?

19. It is useless to vote in municipal elections because our leaders are pre-selected by the Party. Is this true or not?

20. Any citizen of Jalapa who wishes to express himself on important civic matters is free to do so. Do you agree or not?

21. Almost all the decisions in Jalapa are made by a very small group of local people. Do you agree or not?

22. Suppose that someone wanted to give a speech in Jalapa against the Catholic Church and religion. Should he be allowed to do so or not?

23. Suppose that someone wanted to give a speech here in Jalapa against the PRI. Should he be allowed to do so or not?

24. Do you think a member of the Communist Party of Mexico should be allowed to give a speech in Jalapa, or not?

25. In general, are you interested in political affairs? (If the re-

spondent says "Yes," continue.) Would you say that you are very much interested, interested, not very much interested, or not interested at all?

26. At the moment are you a member of any of the following kinds of organizations—unions, peasant organizations, cooperatives, civic organizations, business organizations, religious organizations associated with your church, professional organizations, fraternal organizations (Masons, etc.), or others (which?)?

27. (If the respondent does not belong to any organization, skip to Item 28.) Of these organizations to which you belong, are any related to government affairs, to political or public affairs? For example, do they take part in or discuss political or public issues or try to influence the actions of the government? (If the respondent says "Yes," ask how often.)

28. Now we would like to know something about your preferences for political parties. At the moment are you a member of a political party? (If the respondent says "No," skip to Item 30; otherwise, continue.) Which one?

29. Do you belong to a municipal or state committee of the party?

30. Were you once a member of a political party? Of which one?

31. Would you tell me for which party or presidential candidate you voted in the last two national elections (1964 and 1958)?

32. In the elections for local officials—that is, for those who govern in Jalapa—for which party or candidate for municipal president did you vote in the last two elections (1964 and 1961)?

33. Have you participated actively in any political campaign (making speeches or publicly declaring your support for a candidate? (If the respondent says "Yes," ask how often.)

34. Have you ever gone to an official or functionary of the government here in Jalapa to seek help or support? (If the respondent says "Yes," ask how often.)

35. Have you ever done anything to try to influence a decision related to government affairs in Jalapa? (If the respondent says "Yes," ask how often.)

36. Has any functionary of the government ever contacted you to ask your approval or cooperation in any matter? (If the respondent says "Yes," ask how often.)

Again, I would like to ask you some other kinds of questions. I have here some statements that people sometimes make, and we would like to know what you think about them.

37. Democracy is the best form of government. Do you agree or not?

38. Public officials should be chosen by majority vote. Do you agree or not?

39. Every citizen should have an equal chance to influence government policy. Do you agree or not?

40. The minority should be free to criticize majority decisions. Do you agree or not?

41. The minority should be free to try to influence the opinions of the majority. Do you agree or not?

42. In reality, nobody cares what happens to anybody else. Is this true, partially true, or not true?

43. Most people who do not succeed fail to do so because they lack personal motivation. Is this true, partially true, or not true?

44. People should be better acquainted with new ideas, even though these ideas are contrary to the traditional Mexican way of life. Is this true, partially true, or not true?

45. Some people say that political problems are so complicated and difficult that the average citizen cannot understand them. In general, do you think this is true, partially true, or not true?

46. Insults to one's honor should be forgotten. Is this true, partially true, or not true?

47. One can only trust those whom one knows well. Is this true, partially true, or not true?

48. It is said that certain persons or groups have a lot of influence in running the government, influence that they use to their own advantage while forgetting the well-being of the city. Would you say this is true, partially true, or not true?

49. The majority of our social problems would be resolved if we could eliminate the mental incompetents and the thieves. Is this true, partially true, or not true?

50. All the candidates make beautiful speeches, but one never knows what they will do after they come to power. Is this true, partially true, or not true?

51. In general, are you satisfied with the way you live today? Would you say that you are well satisfied, satisfied, dissatisfied, or highly dissatisfied?

52. Thinking of your economic situation in general—that is, the money that you or your family earns—are you satisfied or not?

53. How do you think your economic situation will change in the next ten years? Will it get better, stay the same, or get worse?

54. How much economic progress do you think Mexico—that is, the entire nation—is making—a great deal, a little, almost none, or none? (If the respondent says "None" or "Don't know" or gives no answer, skip to Item 56.)

55. Personally, how much are you benefiting from this progress—a great deal, a little, very little, or not at all?

56. How much social progress—that is, in education, workers' rights, etc.—do you think Mexico (as an entire nation) is making—a great deal, a little, almost none, or none? (If the respondent says "None" or "Don't know" or gives no answer, skip to Item 58.)

57. Personally, how much are you benefiting from this progress—a great deal, a little, very little, or not at all?

58. In your personal opinion, are basic economic and social changes necessary in Mexico for the country to develop as it should?

59. Would you favor or oppose a land-reform program that would divide the large agricultural properties in order to distribute the land among the peasants? (If the respondent says "Favor," continue.) Do you think that the former owners, those from whom the land is expropriated, should be compensated in full, in part, or not at all?

60. Would you favor or oppose government expropriation—that is, confiscation—of the property of foreigners? (If the respondent says "Favor," continue.) Do you think that the foreign owners should be compensated for their property in full, in part, or not at all?

61. Do you think the difference between people of high economic position—that is, the rich—and people of low economic position—that is, the poor—is much greater than it ought to be, greater than it ought to be, more or less as it ought to be, or less than it ought to be?

I have here a list of statements about human life and political activity in general. I am going to read them to you and would like you to indicate your level of agreement or disagreement with each of these statements. [Response categories for Items 62–70 are Agree completely, More or less agree, More or less disagree, and Disagree completely.]

62. People help each other not so much because they are motivated by a feeling of justice but because they hope to profit personally.

63. Our electoral system is very just and honest.

64. Political activity exposes one to a great deal of unpleasantness and dirt.

65. The most necessary thing for young people is strict parental discipline.

66. In general, the government applies the laws fairly.

67. There are only two kinds of people in the world: the weak and the strong.

68. The government should own all industry and control the entire economic life of the country.

69. It isn't a good idea to let your friends know everything about your life, because they can then take advantage of you.

70. Every politician is a crook.

71. Would you say that most people generally help others, or that they generally are preoccupied with themselves and nothing else?

72. If a man is unemployed, who has the chief responsibility for finding work for him? He himself, his friends and relatives, or the government?

73. Do you think that a man can believe in Communism and still be a loyal Mexican, or not?

74. What do you think about limiting the number of children by means of contraceptives in order for the parents to have children when they want them? Do you approve or disapprove of the use of contraceptives?

75. Do you think the government ought to suppress newspapers and magazines that present an unfavorable picture of life in Mexico, or not?

76. Do you think the voting law should be changed so that only men have the right to vote?

77. Do you think the voting law should be changed so that only those who can read and write have the right to vote?

78. Some people say that you can trust most people. Others say you should distrust most people. What do you think about this?

79. How old are you?

80. What was the last year of school you completed?

81. What is your occupation? (Probe and put down a specific answer.)

82. What is your marital status?

83. What was the last year of school that your father completed?

84. Concerning your religious ideas, do you belong to some religion or religious group? (If the respondent says "Yes," ask which one; otherwise, skip to Item 86.)

85. Approximately how many times each month do you attend religious services?

86. (Show Card #2.) Would you please classify your monthly income in one of these nine groups—less than 500 pesos, 500 to 999 pesos, 1,000 to 2,999 pesos, 3,000 to 3,999 pesos, 4,000 to 5,999 pesos, 6,000 to 7,999 pesos, 8,000 to 12,000 pesos, 13,000 pesos or more?

[At the end of the interview, the interviewer is asked to evaluate the respondent's facility with the language as very good, average, or poor, and his attitude during the interview as friendly, anxious to help; cooperative but reserved; indifferent, cautious; or hostile.]

Elite-Informant Questionnaire

1. Where were you born?
2. How old are you?
3. How long have you lived in Jalapa?
4. Have you lived outside Jalapa for any length of time? (If the respondent says "Yes," ask where.)
5. Do you devote much of your time to city affairs or problems? (If the respondent says "Yes," continue.) Do you regard this intervention as one of your principal activities?
6. How do you get most of your information about city affairs in Jalapa—from what sources and in what form? (If "conversations" are mentioned, continue.) With what type or types of people or with whom do you talk? Generally, where do these conversations take place?
7. Now think about problems of the past. I would like to identify local problems that have received community attention during the last ten years and that have been resolved. What do you think have been the most important problems and needs that have confronted this community during the last ten years and that by now have been resolved one way or another? (The respondent is encouraged to give any number of problems, with approximate dates.)
8. Now think about problems that have not been resolved. Consider the city's needs and problems—things that are needed by the people in Jalapa. What do you believe are the most important problems and needs among those the community must now confront? (Again, any number.)
9. Are there persons or groups in the city who in general are discontented with the management of local affairs or with the way the city is governed? (If the respondent says "Yes," ask who the people are specifically and what their complaints are, and probe for further names; if he says "No," persist.) Do you mean to say that there is no discontent or political conflict in Jalapa? (Probe.)

I would like to discuss with you the reconstruction of Madero Street in 1964.

10. How important did you consider this project for its effect on the community?
11. Did you participate *actively* in the project—that is, did you

actively try to influence its outcome? (If the respondent participated actively, ask 12a–h and then go to Item 14; if he did not, go to Item 13.)

12a. What persons do you believe had considerable influence in the resolution of this affair and why? I am looking for names of people, private citizens as well as officials, who you think were influential.

12b. With what persons were you personally in contact when they were actively participating in this affair? (The respondent is encouraged to give specific names.)

12c. Were these activities organized in any way? That is, did the people who actively participated in the Madero Street project organize themselves in a group or groups for that goal, or were they concentrated in any organization or organizations. (If the respondent says "Yes," probe.) Can you tell me a little more about that? Which organizations were they? Were there any others? (Be sure to find out about activity on all sides of the affair.)

12d. How and when did this need first come to be regarded as important and receive community attention? (Probe.) What persons or groups first drew attention to it, and how?

12e. At what stage did you begin to take part in the affair, and how did this come about? (Probe.) Who first talked to you personally about it? And why were you so chosen? Did you consult any friends or other special persons before deciding to act? (If the respondent says "Yes," ask who.)

12f. What was the nature of your personal participation in the Madero Street project? That is, what were the different kinds of activities that you yourself undertook relating to this affair? (Probe.) Do you remember any people you contacted about it? (If the respondent says "Yes," continue.) Who were they, and what did you want from each one? How successful were these contacts?

12g. Did you consider as highly important in this matter the support of any special sector or sectors of the general public? (If the respondent says "No," ask why not; if he says "Yes," continue.) Which sector or sectors and why? Did you solicit the support of that sector or of those sectors? (If the respondent says he did, ask when and how; if he says he did not, ask why not.)

12h. Did you encounter any difficulties when trying to intervene in this matter? (Probe.) Were there persons or groups who you believed obstructed the solution of the problem? (If the respondent says "Yes,'" continue.) Who were they, and how did they obstruct the solution of the problem? Why did they act that way? Was there any controversy regarding this affair? (If the respondent says there was, ask what kind.)

13a. What persons do you believe had considerable influence in the resolution of the Madero Street project, and why? I am looking for names of people, private citizens as well as officials, who you think were influential.

13b. How and when did this need first receive community attention? (Probe.) What persons or groups first drew attention to it, and how?

13c. What can you tell me about this problem? How was it resolved? (Probe.) Was there any controversy concerning it?

[Items 14, 15, 16, and 17, omitted here, repeat the preceding questions concerning another project, the repaving of Carranza Avenue in 1964. The following items (18–23) relate to a problem or need currently existing in Jalapa—the implementation of city planning.]

18. Which persons do you think could be very influential in the resolution of this problem? I am looking for names of individuals, officials as well as private citizens, who you believe are capable of exerting influence in resolving it.

19. Are there any groups or organizations that could be influential in putting city planning into effect? (If the respondent says there are, continue.) Specifically, which have the resources or the power to influence the resolution of this problem?

20. (Ask if the government is not mentioned in Item 19.) Could the government do anything about city planning? (If the respondent says "Yes," ask specifically what agencies or departments he means; if he says "No," ask why not.)

21. With respect to things like city planning, suppose that the state government were to make a decision affecting the city of Jalapa. Which persons in the city—that is, persons who are not now working for the state government—would have the most influence or the best contacts in state government circles? I am looking for specific names.

22. And which persons in this city would have the most influence or the best contacts in federal government circles regarding affairs or problems in Jalapa such as city planning? That is, persons who are now working neither for the federal government nor for the state government. I am looking for specific names.

23. (Ask this question only of those respondents who have said they are familiar with Jalapan city planning.) I would like to know more about this question. Can you tell me to what extent this question now affects life in Jalapa? That is, what aspects of community life are affected and what, if anything, needs to be done about it.

24. Do any people (of whatever type) who are interested in city affairs sometimes come to talk with you about Jalapa's problems and

needs in order to see whether something can be done? (If the respondent says "Yes," ask what kinds of problems and needs people talk with him about; and if more than one kind, about which they talk most often.)

25. Suppose a person wanted to be a leader in this city. Can you give me some ideas about the things he would have to do and what he would need in order to reach that goal? (If clarification is required, continue.) Would this person have to belong to any organizations or clubs? (The respondent should specify.) Is there anything that this person definitely should *not* be or do? (Again, the respondent should specify.)

26. In the last five years have you *actively* participated in the handling of any important community affairs? (If the respondent says "Yes," continue.) In which ones? Any others? Were you collaborating with other people in these activities? (If the respondent says he was, ask with what type or types of people—for example, government employees, labor leaders, etc.) Has this activity in city affairs been related to your association with any organization or other kind of group? (If so, ask which.)

27. Do you usually deal with people high in the government or in a political party's hierarchy when handling problems and needs of Jalapa—that is, state or federal hierarchies? (If the respondent says "Yes," go to Item 28 and then to Item 30; otherwise, skip to Item 29.)

28a. With what types of people do you usually discuss these problems and needs? (Probe.) Do they work in the government? In what branches or departments? Do they belong to any political party or any other kind of organization? (If so, ask which.)

28b. With what kinds of needs and problems are these contacts concerned? And what are you looking for in these contacts? (Probe for kinds of resources desired or transferred.)

28c. Generally, as they relate to the solution of Jalapa's problems and needs, would you say that these contacts are useful or not useful? That is, do you feel that they accomplish something toward resolving the city's problems? Why?

29a. Have you ever done anything to influence a state decision relating to Jalapa? (If so, ask what.)

29b. Have you ever tried to influence a federal decision relating to Jalapa? (If so, ask what.)

Suppose the state government were considering an act or rule that you considered very unjust or harmful for Jalapa.

30. What do you think you could do about this?

31. If you were to try to change this rule, how much success do you think you could have?

Suppose the federal government were considering an act or rule that you considered very unjust or harmful for Jalapa.

32. What do you think you could do about this?

33. If you were to try to change this rule, how much success do you think you could have?

34. Generally, what do you believe is the actual role of the municipal government in Jalapa? Is the ayuntamiento playing a leading role in any important sectors of community life? (If the respondent says "Yes," ask which sectors and how; if he says "No," ask why not.)

35. I would like to know your opinion about the strengths and weaknesses that exist in the *system* of municipal government in Jalapa; that is, the institution rather than any ayuntamiento in particular. What strengths and weaknesses do you observe? What would need to be done to improve this institution in Jalapa—the municipal government? (If a change is mentioned, continue.) Is this change probable now?

36. In general, what is the actual role of the Junta de Mejoramiento in Jalapa? Is this body playing a significant role in any important sectors of community life? (If the respondent says it is, ask what sectors and how; if not, ask why not.)

(Invite the respondent to make any additional comments about whatever he feels is relevant.)

Conduct of the Research

We spent the latter months of 1965 and the first part of 1966 together in Mexico City planning the study. Tuohy moved to Jalapa in April 1966, arriving with a nearly completed elite-informant questionnaire. He also carried letters of introduction from an ex-Jalapeño to a high state official (his brother), to the then secretary of the ayuntamiento, and to the director of one facultad of the state university. Tuohy soon moved into a pension that was, by good fortune, also the home of an aide to a deputy in the state legislature.

The first weeks in Jalapa were spent getting acquainted with Jalapeños and with local affairs. On the basis of preliminary interviews, a number of local cases and issues were selected for inclusion in the elite questionnaire. Friends helped polish the completed questionaire and then arranged for pre-test interviews in the nearby city of Coatepec. In June 1966 formal interviewing began in Jalapa.

Fifty-five people were formally interviewed at least once as part of the elite study (this total does not include numerous other individuals with whom less formal and less extensive conversations were held). Initially, during June and July, nineteen informants—most selected because they held or had held key positions in state or local government—were interviewed using the full elite questionnaire. In most of these cases, contact was first made through a mutual friend or a previous informant. Each of the nineteen interviews was tape recorded (two were so long that they required two sessions). Assurances of anonymity were given, no interviewee's name was placed on the tape, transcriptions were made soon afterward, and all tapes were then erased.

After these nineteen interviews it became apparent that much of the information still needed was either being missed altogether or being tapped only by certain sections of the questionnaire. Furthermore, despite its obvious utility, the tape recorder inhibited some informants when politically sensitive topics arose. Thus in the subsequent thirty-six interviews a slightly less formal (sometimes abridged, sometimes elaborated) version of the full questionnaire was used, and the informants' responses were not recorded but reconstructed from memory and notes as soon as the interviews were over. Contacted in this second wave of interviewing were not only others who held or had held important state and local offices but also people who, official position aside, were widely regarded and recommended to us as "knowledgeables."

Our elite-informant group included only five women—four university professors and one member of the state government. Among informants actually holding an official position at the time of their interviews were six state officials and bureaucrats, one official in the state organization of the PRI, the then mayor and two other ayuntamiento members (or staff), four members of the Junta de Mejoramiento and its staff, one federal official, and three personal aides to important políticos.[1] Among those holding no official position but considered well informed about community affairs were five newspapermen, eight businessmen, ten members of the university faculty or administration, two university students, and three labor union leaders. Overlapping these two classifications was that of the former holders of official positions—five in the state and one in the federal government, one official in the state PRI, five former mayors and four ayuntamiento members (or staff), and nine who had served on the Junta de Mejoramiento or its staff.

Eleven of the elite informants were lawyers by training, five were engineers, and others held professional degrees in economics, agronomy, psychology, anthropology, architecture, and medicine. A total of thirty-one were licensed professionals.

With few exceptions, interviews took place in the informants' offices; all were conducted in Spanish. Interview time varied considerably, from a minimum of 45 minutes up to several hours. Only a very few potential informants flatly refused to be interviewed, and, given the political sensitivity of the research and the time pressures on most prominent Jalapeños, the generosity and openness of those who did respond were most gratifying.

Less successful was a second, and broader, wave of elite inter-

---

[1] These figures reflect only a single official position for each informant (his post most relevant to our study). Several, however, held more than one office. Most pertinent here, one Junta member was also a state bureaucrat, and three state officials were also state PRI officials.

viewing attempted in September. Using a slightly modified, self-administered version of the citizen questionnaire, Tuohy attempted to interview a wide cross section of Jalapan elites in order to gather data on elite political culture. This time the interviewees were being approached not as informants knowledgeable about the community, its past, and its problems, but rather as members of a larger population being studied. Despite guarantees of anonymity, the questionnaire was perceived as too personal in its probing for details of political beliefs. At the same time, its multiple-choice questions were considered too impersonal. Twelve officers of the Chamber of Commerce, seven labor union officials, and a few others—businessmen, professionals, and friends in the state bureaucracy—did complete and return the questionnaire, but that was all. Understandably, the politicians balked. The attempt to do formal research on elite political culture ceased at that point.

The other major data base for our study of Jalapa consists of interviews with 399 adult Jalapeños. During October 1966, using our citizen questionnaire as developed and pre-tested, International Research Associates of Mexico City did the sampling and interviewing. The universe of potential respondents was defined as all adults (21 years of age or over) residing in the metropolitan area of Jalapa. The most recent available block map of the city was used to select 72 blocks at random. Then a complete list of households on each of the chosen blocks was compiled. Households were then randomly selected within blocks, except that blocks clearly inhabited by people from the upper and upper-middle economic levels were oversampled by a factor of three. Specific respondents were selected in each house by means of a table of random numbers. The research budget allowed for an initial visit to each home and one call-back to locate missing respondents. Interviewing was completed in a week. One interviewer was arrested "for suspicious behavior" (asking suspicious questions), but quickly released. The total cost of the commercially commissioned part of the survey was $2,320 (paid by a Ford Foundation grant).

Weighting the Citizen Sample

The distribution by economic level[2] of the original ($N = 399$) sample was skewed by intentionally oversampling the upper sector: upper sector, 24.8 percent; middle sector, 37.1 percent; lower sector, 38.1 percent. The distribution by sex of the original sample was also skewed (a consequence of unintentionally oversampling women in

[2] This was estimated by those who drew the sample and did the interviewing.

all sectors): 258 women and 141 men. The sample was first weighted to achieve the proper balance between men and women:

Economic level	Orig. male N	$\times$	Weight- ing factor	$=$	New male N	$+$	Orig. female N	$=$	New N
Upper	30		2.33		70		69		139
Middle	56		1.63		91		92		183
Lower	55		1.77		97		97		194

The resulting N was then weighted to achieve the approximate distribution by economic level of the community as a whole:

Economic level	Target per- centage	New N	$\times$	Weight- ing factor	$=$	Final N	Final per- centage
Upper	8.5%	139		1		139	8.9%
Middle	41.5	183		3.5		641	41.2
Lower	50.0	194		4.0		776	49.9
TOTAL	100.0%					1,556	100.0%

This weighting procedure, although somewhat unconventional, offers two analytical advantages. First, it preserves (and only slightly inflates) our original 99 interviews with upper-economic-level respondents, thus giving some statistical reliability to our subsequent statements about these respondents. If we had used a straight probability sample in Jalapa, we would have had only about 30 respondents in this category (and possibly only about 9 men), clearly too few on which to base reliable generalizations. Second, it enables us to make reasonably accurate statements about the community as a whole or about entire social classes. Men differ sufficiently from women on almost all variables so that a sample containing almost twice as many women as men is bound to misrepresent the population in important ways. We can be reasonably sure that our statements about Jalapeños in general (or about any given social class) are not badly skewed by sex-related differences. On the other hand, of course, it is almost impossible to control or estimate error in an inflated sample of this kind. This is one reason why we have used only the most basic kinds of statistical analyses and have sought to carry our argument wherever possible by non-statistical means.

Constructing Scales and Indexes

Class Index. In addition to data on occupation and education (both impossible to use as indexes of class position or social stratification in a sample containing so many housewives), the citizen questionnaire contained two other possible data sources for constructing an index of social class: the interviewer's judgmental estimate of family socio-economic status (SES) based on observations of home furnishings, dress, neighborhood, etc.; and the respondent's statement of total monthly family income. The Spearman product-moment correlation (*r*) between these two variables in the total Jalapa sample was .60. Because of this relatively moderate correlation, it was decided to construct a class index by combining scores on the two variables.

The nine-point income classification was collapsed into three categories: high (3,000 pesos or more), medium (1,000 to 2,999 pesos), and low (999 pesos or less). Scores on income were then combined with scores on judgmental SES in the following manner to produce a class-ranking score for each respondent:

Income	SES	Class ranking
High	High	1
High	Medium	2
Medium	High	3
Medium	Medium	4
Medium	Low	5
Low	Medium	6
Low	Low	7

The correlation of this new class index with education is .61 and with occupation, .54. Throughout the analyses in the body of the book, the class ranking has been trichotomized by combining scores one through three (upper class) and four through six (middle class), and leaving rank seven as it is (lower class). In justification of this procedure it should be noted that the resulting division correlates more strongly with almost all other analytical variables (orientations, behavior) than does either income or SES alone. Also, by letting income data take precedence over SES (when they are not the same) in establishing class-ranking scores, some judgmental errors on the part of interviewers are undoubtedly corrected. The major drawback of the class index is that the full analytical *N* of 1,556 is reduced by 140 because of missing data on income.

Negativism Scale. This is a Guttman scale ordering negativism toward politics. The coefficient of reproducibility is .900; scalability of respondents is .691; scalability of items is .658. Items are here presented in the order in which they appear in the scale: from fewest to most negative responses. Negative responses are scored as ones; other responses are scored as zeros. Scores range from six (highly negative) to zero (not negative at all).

(63)[3] Our electoral system is very just and honest.
　Score of 1
　　Disagree completely
　　More or less disagree
　Score of 0
　　Agree completely
　　More or less agree
　　Don't know
　　No answer
(66) In general, the government applies the laws fairly.
　Score of 1
　　Disagree completely
　　More or less disagree
　　Don't know
　　No answer
　Score of 0
　　Agree completely
　　More or less agree
(64) Political activity exposes one to a great deal of unpleasantness and dirt.
　Score of 1
　　Agree completely
　Score of 0
　　More or less agree
　　More or less disagree
　　Disagree completely
　　Don't know
　　No answer
(70) Every politician is a crook.
　Score of 1
　　Agree completely
　　More or less agree

Score of 0
　Disagree completely
　More or less disagree
　Don't know
　No answer
(50) All the candidates make beautiful speeches, but one never knows what they will do after they come to power.
　Score of 1
　　True
　Score of 0
　　Partially true
　　Not true
　　Don't know
　　No answer
(48) It is said that certain persons or groups have a lot of influence in running the government, influence that they use to their own advantage while forgetting the well-being of the people. Would you say that this is true, partially true, or not true?
　Score of 1
　　True
　　Partially true
　Score of 0
　　Not true
　　Don't know
　　No answer

Authoritarianism Scale. This is a Guttman scale ordering authoritarianism as an individual attribute. The coefficient of reproducibility is .913; scalability of respondents is .661; scalability of items is .627. Items are here presented in the order in which they appear in the scale: from fewest to most authoritarian responses. Authoritarian responses are scored as ones; non-authoritarian responses are scored as zeros. Scores range from five (highly authoritarian) to zero (not authoritarian at all).

[3] Numbers in parentheses here refer to item numbers in the citizen questionnaire (Appendix B).

(44) People should be better acquainted with new ideas, even though these ideas are contrary to the traditional Mexican way of life.
Score of 1
  Not true
  Partially true
  Don't know
  No answer
Score of 0
  True
(49) The majority of our social problems would be resolved if we could eliminate the mental incompetents and the thieves.
Score of 1
  True
Score of 0
  Partially true
  Not true
  Don't know
  No answer
(43) Most people who do not succeed fail to do so because they lack personal motivation.
Score of 1
  True

Score of 0
  Partially true
  Not true
  Don't know
  No answer
(67) There are only two kinds of people in the world: the weak and the strong.
Score of 1
  Agree completely
  More or less agree
Score of 0
  More or less disagree
  Disagree completely
  Don't know
  No answer
(65) The most necessary thing for young people is strict parental discipline.
Score of 1
  Agree completely
Score of 0
  More or less agree
  More or less disagree
  Disagree completely
  Don't know
  No answer

Trust-in-People Index. This is a simple summative index. Scores range from six (highly trustful) to zero (highly distrustful).

(78) Some people say that you can trust most people. Others say that you should distrust most people. What do you think about this?
Score of 1
  You can trust them
Score of 0
  Ought to distrust them
  Depends
  Don't know
  No answer
(71) Would you say that most people generally help others, or that they generally are preoccupied with themselves and nothing else?
Score of 1
  Generally help

Score of 0
  Preoccupied with themselves
  Depends
  Don't know
  No answer
(62) People help each other not so much because they are motivated by a feeling of justice but because they hope to profit personally.
Score of 1
  Disagree completely
  More or less disagree
Score of 0
  Agree completely
  More or less agree
  Don't know
  No answer

(69) It isn't good to let your friends know everything about your life, because they can take advantage of you.
Score of 1
Disagree completely
More or less disagree
Score of 0
Agree completely
More or less agree
Don't know
No answer
(47) One can only trust those whom one knows well.
Score of 1
Not true

Score of 0
True
Partially true
Don't know
No answer
(42) In reality, nobody cares what happens to anybody else.
Score of 1
Not true
Score of 0
True
Partially true
Don't know
No answer

Political Efficacy Scale. Two things about this scale should be noted here: first, it is intended to measure low efficacy; second, it is what might be called a quasi-Guttman scale. There are six items in the scale; however the last two items are contingent on Item three. Thus there is a forced, perfect scale of three items, a fact that serves to inflate the coefficient of reproducibility for the six-item scale. The coefficient of reproducibility is .941; scalability of respondents is .810; scalability of items is .641. The coefficients for the four independent items alone (5, 6, 7, and 45) are: reproducibility, .904; scalability of respondents, .731; scalability of items, .595. Items are here presented in the order in which they appear in the scale: from fewest to most low-efficacy answers. Low-efficacy answers are scored as ones, higher-efficacy answers are scored as zeros.

(6) Speaking of the local problems here in Jalapa, how well can you understand them?
Score of 1
Not at all
Score of 0
Very well
Well
More or less well
Don't know
No answer
(45) Some people say that political problems are so complicated and difficult that the average citizen cannot understand them.

Score of 1
True
Score of 0
Partially true
Not true
Don't know
No answer
(7) Suppose a law or regulation that you considered very unjust or prejudicial to your interests or to the interests of people like yourself were being considered by the municipal government of Jalapa. Do you think you could do anything about it?

Score of 1
   No
Score of 0
   Yes
   Don't know
   No answer
(5) Can you yourself do anything to solve this problem (the problem respondent has identified as the major one in Jalapa)?
   Score of 1
      No, cannot do anything
   Score of 0
      Yes, can do something
      Depends
      Don't know
      No answer

(8) If such a case actually arose, how probable is it that you would really do something to try to change it?

All responses coded "1" for purposes of this scale (question not asked unless respondent answered "yes" to Item 7).

(9) If you were to make an effort to change this law or regulation, how probable is it that you would be successful?

All responses coded "1" for purposes of this scale (question not asked unless respondent answered "Very probable," "Probable," or "Improbable" to Item 8).

Index

Index